THE AESTHETIC SENSE
OF LIFE

A Philosophy of the Everyday

Bruce Fleming

University Press of America,® Inc.
Lanham · Boulder · New York · Toronto · Plymouth, UK

Table of Contents

Preface   v

Chapter One
Individual and General   *1*

Chapter Two
The Aesthetic Sense Inside   *15*

Chapter Three
Public Rhythms   *35*

Chapter Four
The Aesthetic Sense Outside   *51*

Chapter Five
Transitions   *95*

Chapter Six
Religion, Science, and the Aesthetic Sense   *111*

Chapter Seven
Modernity and the Aesthetic Sense   *133*

Chapter Eight
Achieving Goals, Sort Of   *147*

Index   165

About the Author   171

Preface

MATISSE SPOKE OF HIS COLLAGE CUT-OUTS, which he made by painting huge sheets of paper in bright hues, cutting the paper into shapes and arranging them into artworks, as "cutting into color." *The Aesthetic Sense of Life* is the attempt to cut directly into the color of life. Too much philosophy is philosophy of the laboratory: indeed the act of philosophizing has in the twentieth and now twenty-first century come to mean a precise, regulated, way of going about solving problems, which have to be posed in a particular way. Frequently our concern for following the rules of this particular way of considering the world makes us miss the very things that are most important about life: that it is fraught with shifts, constant pullings-out of the rug from under our feet, and that the resultant sense of constantly having to pick ourselves up again is, most essentially, the taste of life.

Some few people, by contrast, have been well aware of the changeability of life: too aware, perhaps, concluding—with Heraclitus—that all is flow. But life isn't more essentially flow than the things that flow, which can include large islands of solidity. In fact, we can't say what the proportion of water to land will be. We may think we're being profound, for example, by insisting that all great civilizations fall. But does this mean our time is up next year? In a millennium? If we give ourselves an infinite period to have a prophecy come true, we will always be right. In the meantime, many things will have happened. History is not more the process of civilizations falling than of their subsisting, nor life more change than stability. The aesthetic sense of life lets us articulate these shifts from one thing to another, and many things in between.

How, otherwise, do we deal with the fact that we are in the middle of things, yet constantly trying to pull ourselves out of this position from which we cannot possibly hope to see the big picture? Conceptualization alternates, and not regularly, with situations where conceptualization is impossible; the certain takes its place alongside the uncertain. *The*

Aesthetic Sense of Life offers, as the sub-title suggests, "A Philosophy of the Everyday." In echoing Unanumo's celebrated *Tragic Sense of Life*, it suggests that the particular content of life varies, it's the attitude we take toward this that remains constant—and gives life its taste. The aesthetic sense is a way of approaching life, a perspective that allows us both to deal with the times when the rug is pulled from under us, and the times when it is fixed. Each is what it is; life is not more insecure than secure, nor the reverse.

The aesthetic sense as a way of approaching life lies between two extremes, the religious extreme that's completely uninterested in the sights, tastes, and sounds of the world, on one hand; on the other the extremely worldly that is incapable of questioning any detail of the sensuous world, all of which seems inevitable to the person experiencing them. It results neither in the "life is chaff" abnegation of the truly religious, nor in the "whatever happens is good" immersion in particulars of the truly worldly. (These two positions, strangely enough, close the circle when they combine to produce the conviction that God meant all this to happen to me because I am who I am.) The aesthetic sense of life acknowledges that particulars are merely particulars, nothing more than themselves, but insists that given enough time, they arrange themselves into patterns that give meaning to the whole. The aesthetic sense of life is the willingness to let this arrangement happen, even though we ourselves are part of the life that is rearranged. We do what we do, and later look behind us to see what that was. Thus the aesthetic sense of life is reactive in an intellectual sense: we have to wait and see what happens before we can try and understand it. But that acknowledges that the world is greater than we are: it contains us. We are part of the patterns that form.

The aesthetic sense of life allows us to be both engaged in life, and detached from it, both driving our lives and riding shotgun on them. It allows us to be aware of the unity of the self throughout our lives, and the vast changes that happen to us and by us along the way: it's not clear that we're more unified than disparate, more ourselves than amalgams of other people.

The aesthetic sense of life, finally, helps us celebrate the minutia of our lives without thinking them overly important. The petty details of anyone's life constitute the reality of that life, in the same way that the molecules of our bodies are, ultimately, us. Yet at the same time, we act in the world, do the things that others cannot do, by moving these molecules in specific ways: the aesthetic sense of life teaches us to celebrate both the details and the patterns of meaning they assume.

For the perfectly individual cannot be shared, and cannot be used to create meaning in life. Unless we can see how what is particular about us

links to other people, we are condemned to one of the two extreme
flanking the aesthetic sense of life: either details matter absolutely, ii
which case we are prisoners of our lives, or they don't matter at all, ii
which case we stop our senses to the world and think only of a highe
realm, or of a subsequent life. The aesthetic sense of life allows us to see
the millions of tiny sense impressions of which our lives are composec
both as ends in themselves, things to celebrate—the taste of a fruit, th
color of a sunset, the rustle of a leaf—and means to an end of providin
meaning for our lives as they configure into patterns, things we can shar
with others, the rustling body of our lives like veils shaken by ai
oncoming storm from which a sense of meaning with respect to others i
constructed.

Annapolis, Maryland
July 25, 2007

Chapter One
Individual and General

MANY PEOPLE, SOONER OR LATER, come to the conclusion that life lacks any overarching point—at least, that it lacks a point we can be sure about, or prove, or get in any other way than simply by accepting it from a guru or priest. Such people conclude that if we don't find value in what life feels and tastes like from within without asking what it's *for*, we're not going to get very much from it. Such tastes and feels are readily available, if only we pay attention to them. We live on the surface of life, which is composed of constantly slipping, very small tectonic plates. The concentration on the slipping of the miniature tectonic plates that produces constant small tremors in us is living with what I call the aesthetic sense of life.

Zoom lens

The aesthetic sense of life is a particular focus of the zoom lens through which we perceive the world. It's a setting in the middle, so one of the most efficient ways of initially defining this sense of life is by contrast with the two extremes that flank it, one on each side of the middle focus.

On one extreme is the setting of the people completely, and perhaps happily, married to the world; at the other extreme are those all but divorced from it—complete divorce being possible only with death. In the middle, the aesthetic sense of life, is the setting of those who, to quote Robert Frost's gravestone, have a "lover's quarrel with life."

On the one side of the setting for the aesthetic sense of life is the setting of those who see a series of detailed close-ups: the camera registers individual details, discrete factoids. The mechanism of getting from one to another of these details is not itself amenable to consideration. People living at this setting don't conceive of the relationships between individual details as being something that's amenable to codification: each bit of the world is absolute. To be sure, they're not without a mechanism for unpeeling themselves from the flow of sensations that come their way, but they can't conceptualize this focusing and the choice involved in it except as individual, something that isn't amenable to justification or explanation. They can change from one detail to another and may do so repeatedly; what they don't accept is that consideration of this change is possible, or that the process of change itself can be seen from the outside.

These people are bonded to the world, taken over by things as they are. Such people are the extremely worldly, though not in the sense of sophisticated—rather, in the sense of an alternative to religious. Those not at this setting would say: What such people lack is the ability to ask why they move from detail to detail. Such people believe that whatever they have is what they were meant to have; whatever they are is what they were meant to be. What is, in short, is inevitable. To themselves, they seem resolute and focused; to an outsider they seem maddeningly smug and frustratingly unquestioning.

In political terms, people at this focus setting are natural conservatives. For them, the world consists solely of the details, not the relationship between them, which is up to individual choice. What they focus on can only be justified by the one-size-fits-all explanation of their having focused on it. This, cumulatively, is choice, and in their view they are the last great individualists. By definition, others can't convince these people that any things play a role in who they are than merely their individuality, which is as it is and is not amenable to further codification: not society, not their family, not sexuality, not natural endowments, not any identifiable thing. Identifying such things that determine the individual is tantamount to denying the complete freedom of that individual to chart his or her own destiny.

A natural horror

Abortion is a natural horror for such people who take the world as it is for granted. They perceive each "what if?" scenario which suggests that the people who exist *might not have been* as an attack on them personally. A typical reaction to someone who says that a fetus can be intentionally de-railed on its way to birth is: "Are you saying I shouldn't have been born?" If we say, "Certainly it's *possible* you might not have been born, or me," this typically causes apoplexy. Not because it isn't true, but because such thinking is profoundly at odds with this setting of the zoom lens. It suggests that we can introduce contingency into the marriage of self and world that is at the core of this setting.

The possibility that the person *might not have been* is an even more fundamental attack on this setting than the suggestion that we can begin to say something in general terms about the change from detail to detail, from precise given to precise given, other than leaving it open to the wide open spaces of individual "choice." Though such people think themselves in control of their fate, in fact they are controlled by the things that come at them: they are so integrated with the world that they are its prisoners. To say this person might not have been is to say that 100% of what fills the lens might not have been. And that is, the world.

This is the focus setting Voltaire is skewering in his merciless novella *Candide* through views taken out of context from the philosopher Leibnitz. Voltaire gives these to the monotonous Dr. Pangloss, who insists repeatedly that everything is "for the best in this best of all possible worlds." Voltaire's point is not that this position is logically incoherent—in fact, it's a necessary conclusion if we assume the existence of a good and omnipotent God: if God is all-powerful and good, then the world He created must in fact be the best possible, despite the way it seems to us. At the same time clearly it strips people of their imagination, their ability to run alternatives, their sense of "what if?" People like Pangloss, happy at everything because existence is the same as necessity, have no sense of "what if"—they conceive of no viable alternatives to what is. For such people, everything that is was meant to be. If the opposite happens, that was meant to be too.

At the other end of the scale from these natural conservatives are not, as we might expect, natural liberals. These tend to be found in the middle of the scale, in the realm of the aesthetic sense of life. For this reason the liberal/conservative dichotomy is not the one primary to my consideration here; for a development of this conflict see my book *Why Liberals and Conservatives Clash*. No: at the other end of the scale are people who, instead of being married to the world, are instead completely removed from it. These are people with what, for the sake of simplicity, we may call the religious point of view—religion being the means in which this point of view is most commonly expressed.

This religious end of the spectrum comes from blurring our eyes to particulars, to the point where we see only the endless pattern of repetition: we've become so abstract that nothing seems new. Typically, this leads to a sense of alienation from life—the acceptance of religious fatalism perhaps of the Buddhist sort, the feeling that life is intrinsically pain, and the point of life is to escape that pain, which is to say, escape life itself. Or in Christian terms, the insistence that Earthly life is only the brief interlude before the big show, the curtain-raiser that (a bit paradoxically) on one hand is of no intrinsic importance, but actually of paramount importance in determining all the rest.

The *advantages* of using life as a springboard to jumping to another level are clear: we no longer have to deal with the endless murmurings (such as they will seem from a religious point of view) of hope and despair, pain and pleasure—we summarize them all, declare them unworthy, and fill that place with the endless Om of contemplating the That-Which-Does-Not-Change. The clear *disadvantage* of this setting of the zoom lens—one which those who reach this position are willing to accept—is related to its advantage, the fact that this setting of the lens blanks out all the details: it's inhuman, in that its point is to reach a level where the individual human, which otherwise determines life, is of secondary, tertiary, or indeed no importance at all.

Western religion—if there is such a thing, virtually all religions having started in the East—has tended to put a positive spin on this setting of the lens, postulating the achievement of an external, transcendent value, rather than (expressed in negative terms) merely an escape from the endless cycle. Western religion, with its heaven or afterlife, has been sold as life-affirming, rather than life-denying. It's been presented as the meaning of our humanity, this achievement of something outside of us. And this has tended to disguise the fundamentally inhuman nature of even these religions, in the sense that any particular setting of the zoom lens in this part of the scale blanks out the details of life.

Embedded in reality

The religious end of the scale is related to the here and now not because of its theory—which escapes the murmuring of life absolutely—but because of the fact that most people do no more than aim at this setting, without achieving it. Or, more often yet, talk of aiming at it: in fact it's the aiming at this setting, or the contemplation of the aiming at this setting, which is the way this setting is most frequently integrated into life. This is so because a postulation of something beyond life, as Wittgenstein points out in the *Tractatus,* is always part of life. That too is part of the pattern the "something" purports to escape, part of the "ceaseless ebb and flow of human misery," as Matthew Arnold called it (even if we add "joy" to the misery—something Arnold apparently was unaware of—and whose omission limits the applicability of his formulation). We can try to have more of the joy and less of the misery, but in any case going forward presupposes ignoring the misery and emphasizing the joy to the point where we'll never know which really was more prevalent than the other.

The closest setting on this scale to the aesthetic sense of life is related to this transcendent extreme, given that most of us have contact with the transcendent not in achieving it, but in trying (and failing) to achieve it. Housewares stores stock a light bulb meant for outdoor lantern-type fixtures where, once upon a time, there would have been candles: the point of the light bulb is to mimic the flickering of a candle, at least to the passer-by. It achieves this effect by having two filaments shaped roughly in the form of flames between which the light jumps in a not-completely-predictable pattern. The bulb is the endless flickering, as neon signs with arrows are the endless progression of turning on and off different parts of the sign. Many thinkers have concluded that we are in fact such bulbs made to flicker between the here and now and the transcendent at which we aim, and, intermittently, achieve, this the nature of the "human condition."

We are not condemned to this endless striving and failure; the aesthetic sense of life is my attempt to offer an alternative. However the notion of life as the flicker of this bulb, the yearning toward and constant falling away from the transcendent, is a seductive one. John Keats, for one, apparently thought this was in fact the nature of what it meant to be alive. He thought it inevitable that we'd postulate transcendent value—something, he points out, that only creatures on this non-transcendent side of the fence will do. We're the ones postulating it, which means we never achieve it, only postulate achieving it. We're made to flicker.

This is the paradox at the center of Keats's "Ode on a Grecian Urn." The young man (or, the narrator notes, possibly god—he's physically perfect, so we don't really know whether he's mortal or immortal) chasing the female in the first of the urn's two scenes is frozen before the moment of achieving his goal, namely getting the girl (the girl doesn't much like being this young god-man's goal, it seems, she's "loath"). The narrator of the poem realizes that the god-man would probably find this inability to achieve his goal upsetting, but tells him: "Do not grieve." There's good news in this situation, namely that he'll always be in love (lust?) with the woman, because (this is apparently the reason his feelings won't change) she's always going to be beautiful.

This situation is compared to love in the human sphere, where a person can in fact achieve his (or her) goal. This would seem to be good news, a clear advantage of the real world over the world of the urn—until we're told that the result is being "cloy'd," a word typically used with too much of something that's overweeningly sweet. We get so much of it we become sick. In the real world, the boy can get the girl, but then he gets the flu, "a burning forehead and a parching tongue."

It's fun to imagine that this urn, the marble pot Keats is writing about, was an academic class assignment, a response to the prompt "portray perfection." The less talented members of the class probably showed people who had actually achieved their goals, and were wearing the laurel wreath of victory. The maker of this urn, however, realized that the most perfect moment is not the achieving of the goal, rather the moment before its achievement. Achieving the goal is actually the beginning of the inevitable downslide; at least this is how the narrator sees it.

The paradox is that this image of perfection, the urn (or, it later becomes clear, the poem) is made by such imperfect creatures as the real-life men who contrast to the eternally frustrated but eternally interested man on the urn. The narrator of the poem knows we'll never ourselves be the creature on the urn: we're the ones who make urns, not the ones on them. Its world is unlike ours, and we unlike the people portrayed on it. Yet they *are* what we would create, with a little reflection, if told to "portray perfection." Perfection is the not-us: perfection is only attainable in the postulated artificial world of urns and poems, not here on Earth. Yet it's people on Earth who postulate these artificial worlds, the imperfect who create the perfect, even if that means that perfection is limited to such things as urns, poems, and the soaring rhetoric of inspirational speeches. Transcendent meaning transcends, requires, and comes to be as a result of the non-transcendent, the imminent.

So which trumps which? It all seems like a cosmic game of rock/paper/scissors. The way we mutable humans interact with the urn's perfection is the way of the flickering bulb: we may even think we achieve this perfection, but then fall back to Earth with a bump as we realize that we, after all, were the ones who made the pot, wrote the poem, achieved the goal, now behind us.

Stripping gears

Keats offers another flickering bulb as an analogy at the end of the poem. He's trying to give an equivalent to the central paradox of the urn, which is that it's a "Cold Pastoral." Pastorals, poems about spring full of lambs and new growth, are of course warm; this one is cold—it's lifeless, except when it's not (when we add the life, imagine the figures on the urn into life). He compares thinking about the urn, this "cold pastoral," to thinking about eternity. He says thinking about eternity "teases us out of thought." It strips our mental gears; we can't think any more, and are left shaking our head.

Keats doesn't elaborate, but we can: If we're to be eternal, just what exactly does that mean? What part of us? Presumably, what we usually call the "soul" or a comparable term that means only this part or aspect of the human being that survives Earthly life. But what are the qualities of the soul? In order to go beyond this single word used as a technical term, a term with no qualities whose use is merely to say that it's not anything we're familiar with, we have to say more. Those in the Christian tradition have visualized the soul as somehow taking the form of angels with wings (though as a character in Aldous Huxley's *Point*

Counterpoint notes, any person-shaped creature that could fly would need a chest musculature six times that of a human chest). But any particular set of qualities for the soul—here summarized as implying angels—has its own set of problems, raising questions like these: How old are angels? Do they have memories of their previous life? Are they of one sex or another? Do they, in their angel-life, have any attachment to those they knew in the transitory human lives?

Frequently funeral services will include references by the surviving spouse to seeing the departed in the hereafter. But what is it about a soul that will allow another soul to "recognize" it? What if one soul is of a woman who died at 20, or a loved child of 1; the other is the husband or parent who lived to the age of 95? Even if one soul can recognize the other without the body, will the relationship be the same as on the day the first person died? Does a soul another soul knew "look" different than the soul of someone unknown to that soul? The question was sometimes posed this way: How old are souls or angels? Christian theology of the Middle Ages decided that all angels were 33 years old, like Jesus at His death. Even those that died as infants or 90-year-olds? If they have memory of Earth, do the 90-year-olds lose the memories between 33 and 90? Do angels eat? Do they excrete? Do their long white gowns grow dirty from the clouds? And so on. In fact, there really isn't much we can say about what eternity will be like. Are we conscious of it being eternity? What do we do to pass the time (if that's the right word)? Is it merely an eternity of hours? Or is it measured in some other way? Do we sing the same song of praise over and over? Do we get bored with it? Is it eternal time, or suspended time? We don't know.

Depictions of hell have always worked better than depictions of heaven; most people note that they like Dante's *Inferno* better than his *Paradiso*. We can imagine an eternity of torment, wishing it to stop in every moment and in every moment knowing it won't, better than we can an eternity of bliss—perhaps because we're conscious of the passage of time when we want something to stop, pain to go away: hell is clearly endless hours, years, millennia. But heaven? An eternity of good things? An eternity of lack of pain? Or of bliss? Isn't bliss the tip of an iceberg, having meaning only by contrast with the mundane? How can it be eternal?

God will solve these problems, some say. Others add: Of course we can't imagine heaven. We're still on Earth; we're not yet among the Blessed. But that's Keats's point: thinking about eternity on this side, as creatures not among the Blessed (whom we can never visualize from this direction) is a dead end. We give up. Similarly, Keats suggests that thinking about the "cold pastoral" of the urn strips our gears and causes us to give up. Do we achieve transcendence if we're the ones who postulate it? Realizing that the urn does pose a paradox is what pushes us to the aesthetic sense of life, a desire to escape the endless flicker of this hurling ourselves into the transcendent and falling back again and again.

Cutting the Gordian knot

This endless flinging about is a sort of Gordian knot: there's no way to escape it so long as we accept its premises, that our choices are either/or, transcendence or its lack. The aesthetic sense of life cuts this Gordian knot: we're no longer flinging ourselves towards transcendence, though we know we'd like to. Doing so is a sort of defeat, in that we're condemned to fall back again—we're giving in to our impulses.

With the aesthetic sense of life we live life with a purposely limited point of view, aware of small variations, of slippages, of the ways things look and feel, of how they diverge from what they ought to be, change, and are set right again. Seen as an aesthetic experience, life once again becomes full of meaning: seeing another person, say, respect a boundary both of us know to be there gives us pleasure, in that we note the boundary has been respected and understand why the other person has done this. A boundary over-stepped gives us no less pleasure: we realize that the person is doing this for a reason, or perhaps that the person is so dull s/he has no idea s/he has done this. We become aware of our expectations of the normal by nothing things that transgress these: anything out of line with our expectations (a sunset is more lurid than we've ever seen, for example) is interesting to us. A bad movie is as much fun as a good one—more, probably, because we're aware of each shock against probability in the plot, each shot held too long or too relentlessly cut on the dramatic high point, each reaction by the star slightly off-kilter with respect to where it would have to be to be believable. An ill-mannered person is as satisfying to be around as a well-mannered one: we can be aware of each offense against the rules. With luck, it means we laugh at boors: they too take up room. We rub our hands: a new species to categorize!

Leap of faith

The aesthetic sense of life thus rejects as pointless, if understandable, the Keatsian flicker. It also, even more clearly, rejects the leap of faith into the realm of religion—a leap accessible in any case only to a few. Most people only gesture toward the transcendent; a handful of people on the face of the Earth achieve it. The aesthetic sense is an alternative to them as well.

The religious leap of faith solves the problems of mutability, the fact that we rarely get what we want, and when we do we find we're not satisfied, the aching fact that loving somebody doesn't mean we can live for them and spare them any woe, any more than anyone could live our lives for us, or spare us any woe: ours will come to us, as theirs to them. How much pain realizing this causes us! How much pain it causes us to see our children, creatures once dependent on us turn away, given that we have done our job in making them self-sufficient! We know this is what we were to have done, and we have done it: we have made ourselves irrelevant. We now are merely watching from the sidelines. Our time to die will come soon.

Achieving, rather than aiming at, the focus on the zoom lens we associate with religion, is not something most of us can do. Indeed, it's not something we want to do. Or even necessarily something we should want to do. It's awesome, in the literal rather than teen-aged sense: to be able to scoop all of life as we know it—the sights, the smells, the sounds—up in our hands and dump it overboard. Do I really have to give up brie cheese and chardonnay? Yes, if you want to be one with God.

But didn't God make chardonnay too? Aren't we allowed any Earthly pleasures? Or must we be miserable? Not miserable, comes the response: you've thrown away the chaff and kept the wheat, the Heavenly treasure. But the sacrifice seems counter-intuitive to most: why would we even exist in this world if we were supposed to refuse it all and reject it? It seems so life-hating, in a way, rather than life-affirming as it's supposed to be. This is why the achieving of the transcendent, probably limited to saints and sadhus, is something we more typically fall away from, once again trapped in the flicker between the two filaments of the bulb.

Dover Beach

It's clear why we'd be drawn to this flicker in the first place: we realize that life is loss, forgetting, and the process becoming irrelevant. And how glorious it was to be! Of course we'd be inclined to give it up as a bad job. The aesthetic sense of life can be achieved as we weary of the flicker. As Matthew Arnold puts this deception in "Dover Beach": "the world, which seems/ To lie before us like a land of dreams,/ So various, so beautiful, so new,/ Hath really neither joy, nor love, nor light,/ Nor certitude, nor peace, nor help for pain."

Arnold seems to have missed the fact that we can in fact triumph. Only here too the canker lies at the heart of the rose. Let's say we go from triumph to triumph. At some point nobody cares—or worse, people take our triumphs for granted, so that they are part of the definition of who we are, something we do, like breathing. Movie stars don't get credit for being movie stars: that's the nature of who they are. In fact, they're punished if they don't triumph, by smaller salaries and lesser roles. Most of us never even have to try staying on top, because we never get there. Probably we won't be completely unappreciated, but what others praise us for are pale versions of what we'd hoped for. Our choices on receiving this praise are, on one hand, to grin fixedly and accept the compliment, so it seems we have in fact achieved something, or alternately, to explain to everyone how much less we've achieved than we'd hoped—which will simply make them turn away, puzzled at our sourness.

Still, we must somehow cope with the fact that nobody else ever sees the world the way we do. Others can be happy for us, but at some point they are gone from our lives, or we from theirs. And finally everyone of our generation is gone, and (if we were "famous") we have become the two or three photographs or pieces or actions people remember—what a tiny pile is what remains out of all our thoughts and feelings, now gone! Sometimes we say that these now-vanished thoughts and feelings have meaning in God's eyes—which admits they lack it here on Earth. This is like saying that we have no idea what someone will do with the six boxes of clippings and lovingly saved memorabilia we're handing them, but here they are.

Or, on the other hand, we can be alive to the patterns that the raw material of life assumes as we live it. This option leads us to the aesthetic sense of life.

Learning more

We come to the aesthetic point of view as we realize that part of the strangeness of life is certainly that we have the sense of learning more and more and then are unable to pass it on. Everyone else wants to learn things on his or her own too, as we did in our own time. We may leave traces, but others do with them as they choose. Indeed to many others we may be nothing but an impediment to the process of their own discovery, and at our disappearance they are glad they need no longer deal with us. Even as we age, nobody in the next generation will listen to us saying life isn't worth it (to them it is), and if we sit around with those our own age talking about it, we brand ourselves as hopeless old fogies. Clearly mental health lies in taking pleasure in the pleasure of the young: in finding somebody who still believes in Santa Claus to whom we can be Santa Claus rather than bellyaching about the realization that there is no Santa Claus.

Explaining why we end up with the aesthetic sense of life thus involves explaining why we should be at neither of the two states that flank it: neither the state that insists on the possibility of real transcendence on one hand, nor the state that can't conceive of any abstraction greater than the perceived world. The religious alternative colors all particulars with the same tint, so that particular differences are irrelevant. It's un-choosey in the same way the relentlessly worldly point of view, the obverse of the religious, is un-choosey: whatever happens is good for the worldly point of view; for the religious, whatever happens is bad.

The aesthetic sense of life, by contrast with both, requires us to find meaning through relations of particulars. This means that not all particulars will be able to contribute to the construction of meaning. If the aesthetic sense of life is one step back towards the practical from the religious perspective, it's a step toward the abstract with respect to a complete immersion in the flow of life. The aesthetic sense of life involves knowing where we are in the flow but seeing ourselves simultaneously as if from the outside. We live our lives, and then look behind us to see what patterns they made.

Tractatus

My consideration here of the aesthetic sense of life is an attempt to give a viable alternative to the point of view expressed in Wittgenstein's *Tractatus Logico-philosophicus*, proposition 6.41. The *Tractatus* seen as a whole is a meditation on the flickering nature of our striving toward the transcendent. Like Keats, Wittgenstein notes that we constantly try to access a level beyond ourselves—we strive after it, as we might have said in the nineteenth century, but that it is only transcendent with respect to the imminent, the world as it is. What he's emphasizing is that our connection with the transcendent is not the fact that we attain it, but the fact that we aim for it. It's transcendent because it transcends.

This book is a commentary on this situation, because it moves to the next step, answering the implicit question: what are we to do with this information?

The translation of Wittgenstein is mine; it diverges from the standard Pears and McGuinness translation in several important respects to which I turn shortly.

6.41 The sense of the world must lie outside the world. In the world everything is as it is, and everything happens as it happens: there's no value within the world—and if this "value" did exist in the world, it would have no value.

> *If there is any higher value that really does have worth, it must lie*
> *outside everything that exists and that is as it is. For everything that*
> *happens and is is merely what is, the way things are.*
>   *What makes it something other than merely what happens to hap-*
> *pen can't be a part of the world, since if it were in the world, it too*
> *would merely be part of the way things are.*
>   *It would have to lie outside the world.*

Equally, this book is a commentary on *Tractatus* 6.3611. *We cannot*
compare a series of events with 'the passage of time'—there is no such
thing—, only with another series of events (for example with the working
of a timing device).

Before explaining, a note on my translation. In 6.41, where I write
For everything that happens and is is merely what is, the way things are,
Pears and McGuinness write: "All that happens and is the case is accidental." Wittgenstein writes "alles Geschen und So-Sein ist zufällig."
Here Pears and McGuinness are translating "zufällig" as "accidental,"
which it can mean when we speak of meeting some "per Zufall," by accident. But we'd also say, for example, someone is "zufälligerweise" in
town at the same time as us—that's not, in English, "accidentally" in
town at the same time we were there (the person presumably meant to be
there)—but rather simply as the result of the way things are: we'd say
he's there "by chance" at the same time as us, or "coincidentally."

Indeed, it seems odd to speak of the world as "accidental" in English;
this suggests a drowsy demiurge or a distracted God doing something so
to speak with his (His) left hand without paying much attention to it.
Some theologies have held this, but it seems far from Wittgenstein. Wittgenstein doesn't seem to have thought the world was an "accident,"
merely that it was as it was. The opening of the *Tractatus*, after all, is the
celebrated assertion that "The world consists of everything that is." (*Die
Welt ist alles, was der Fall ist.*) In the Pears and McGuinness translation,
this has come down as "The world is everything that is the case." Something "being the case" is reserved in English for statements, which begins
to explain why generations of Anglophone readers have regarded the
Tractatus as primarily a treatise on language. It's the case that someone
is sitting on the chair. Not: someone sitting on the chair, but *that* someone is doing it. It's a statement that's the case, not the thing asserted.

The world for Wittgenstein buzzes with the fact that it's what is: the
world is busy being itself. At the same time that means it's *only* what it
is, not something beyond itself. You can say or do anything in the world,
and what you've done or said won't be beyond the world; it'll merely be
part of the world. It's thus strange that the *Tractatus* was understood for
so long as forbidding people from saying certain things: the Vienna

School of logical positivism that tried to rule out the possibility of ethics, say that certain things we try to say should not, or could not, be said.

This reading, to be sure, seems justified by such sentences as 6.42, a proposition which follows from the long proposition 6.41 I quoted above: "Thus there can't be any statements in ethics." This seems to say: Pile up all those books of ethics and let's burn them! But the next sentence cools our ardor and quells the flames: "Statements can't express anything higher." It's not that we can identify a specific realm of expressions of, say, ethics, or theology, and declare them off limits. It's that anything we thought escaped the world doesn't in fact succeed in doing this. Instead, it merely becomes part of the world. Any further action is irrelevant.

Any expression of point of view, therefore, can interact with those that preceded it, but it's doomed to being merely the next in line that others will interact with. For the person who expresses the point of view, it is the world; for someone following it becomes merely another datum, something subsumed in its turn to another world.

Wherever you go, there you are!

The whole *Tractatus* is a sympathetic look at the human proclivity to try and get around behind our own backs and say things that are more than what we can say. It knows we're going to try and do this: if it weren't more than we could say, why would we try and do it? Its reiterated point is that we are only what we are: try though we might, we'll only be what we are. That doesn't mean we should stop trying to do anything in particular, it's just saying that the result will be reality, not something else. It's an echo of Proust's point in the *Search for Lost Time (Remembrance of Things Past)*, that—in the words of a guidebook to Mexico I've used—"Wherever you go, there you are!" Dreaming of Venice, as the narrator Marcel does in Proust's melancholy masterpiece, isn't the same as getting to Venice, because when you get there you're there—as Wittgenstein would say, you're "tatsächlich" there, you're in the real world, part of what's true. Wherever you go, whatever you do, you're condemned to be in the world of things as they are, not things as they aren't.

Thus man, as a creature, is constantly trying to be something he's not: this is a fair summation too of Sartre's point in *Being and Nothingness*. For Sartre it was solidity that human beings were constantly seeking, Being rather than the eternal Becoming, seeking changelessness rather than the eternal change to which we are otherwise condemned. Wittgenstein might himself point out that nothing in this situation, assuming it's ours, tells us how to react to this. That would be the higher sense that by definition isn't in the world, and so isn't accessible to us: whatever we find is by definition part of the world. In the *Tractatus*, this seems to have led to a sort of contented equanimity:

> *6.45 The view of the world in its eternal aspect (sub specie aeterni) is the view as a whole that nonetheless is limited.*
> *The feeling of the world as limited whole is the mystical feeling.*

Sartre, by contrast, seems to have felt a sense of real insufficiency, of straining after something he couldn't get. For Wittgenstein, the reaction to this realization was more Olympian—the world, after all, seen *sub specie aeterni*: 6.5: "To an answer that we can't articulate, we can't articulate the question either. There's no big riddle." Sartre, by contrast, seems to have been furious that things were this way, the poor human being condemned to becoming trying over and over to turn itself into being, usually through unsavory means—Sartre's dreaded "bad faith," Becoming laboring under the illusion it could be Being, humanity in flight from itself. Sartre's world is populated by ghosts futilely trying to solidify themselves again, like people trying to force themselves into sleep (it can't be done, as Sartre points out). Wittgenstein's is by far the more patrician, less melodramatic attitude.

Here I propose another response to this realization, one that lies in intensity between Sartre's furious "it isn't fair!" and Wittgenstein's "What can you do?" This is what I'm calling the aesthetic sense of life. If we consider the transcendent, as Wittgenstein does, we seem to be obliged to operate in a negative fashion, saying: we can't actually achieve transcendence, only aim for it.

The *Tractatus* is about being satisfied with flinging ourselves again and again, each time futilely, into the void, only to fall back repeatedly with a thump. The aesthetic sense of life no longer flings itself, understanding both the reason for the attempt and its inevitable failure. Thus one way to describe the aesthetic sense of life is a damping down of the *Tractatus*: its conclusion of inevitability without all the histrionics that precede this equanimity (or is it merely exhaustion?).

Seen from this direction, therefore, the aesthetic sense ends up feeling like an especially clear-eyed pessimism—certainly it seems so when compared to those who insist we can in fact achieve the truly transcendent, the religious point of view that Wittgenstein tells us we'll never get. Seen from the point of view of those who are their own particulars, it's not pessimistic: it's just puzzling, or infuriating. For such people there is nothing but particulars, joined by "choice"—and, I consider later, "belief."

Chapter Two
The Aesthetic Sense Inside

ACHIEVING THE AESTHETIC SENSE OF LIFE inside the boundaries of our world involves some degree of decoupling from what we know to be true. It's easier outside those boundaries, a subject to which I turn below. The aesthetic sense of life involves paying attention to life as it unfolds, with us an actor within it, to note the patterns it makes, the structures that come to be. We can't know beforehand what those are. This process can be described at the most general level; beyond that it can only be exemplified, as each person's life is different from every other.

Here's an example from one particular day of allowing the world to form its own patterns: the way the specifics of my world lined up on the day of the Army-Navy football Game, December 2004, the world seen from the perspective of that one moment. In this case the patterns involve the expression of masculinity through war and aggression and how these relate to the private world of the individual, which is composed of countless small and intrinsically insignificant details. Such patterns abruptly become clear in our lives like an alignment of the stars, each of which is doing its own thing: suddenly they are in alignment. And just as quickly as the alignment is achieved, it dissolves; all we can hope for is to have been conscious of it while it lasted and savor it a bit in memory when it is gone.

Army-Navy day 2004, late afternoon

It rained last night, so the white plastic lawn chair speckled with the brown stain I put on the deck last year that fell through the cracks to the level beneath—I hadn't thought of that—has a little pool of water right where my rump has to go. It's cool, and the sun is going down, but Owen has just gotten up from his nap and it's the only time we have to go "ow-tie," as he calls "outside." The swing set was installed a month ago, on a flattened out area of the otherwise sloping back yard, only the area the woman on the phone told us to flatten turned out to be too small—she was only thinking of the size of the set, it turned out, not the area for little bodies to come shooting off the sliding board—and the area has since been enlarged, and the swing set turned on its bed of woodchips. Outside the railroad ties that frame the flattened area the yard is still muddy, the part that isn't covered with leaves that go down to the surprisingly wild-looking woods behind the house. A large tree fell down the slope a few weeks ago. I didn't hear it, and was only aware of such violence so close to the fragile domestic shell of our house when I noticed that the otherwise almost perfectly vertical parallels of the leafless trees was ruined with a sort of diagonal Broadway cutting across them: this, it turned out, was pulled down by the tree that had fallen, that I investigated up close to see a root ball startlingly small for such an endlessly tall tree, spread upended on its side, but still much larger than I am, the roots now snaking out into the air, for them as alien an element as for a fish.

I dump the water off the chair. It leaves a brown slick, and of course is still wet. Owen is involved with making a mess in the mud with his green froggy boots—it's only in the last day or two he's accepted not wearing them all day long, even to sleep, and agrees that the boots too, like Daddy's, belong "ow-tie," especially when they are caked with mud. I dry off the wet spot with some leaves and sit down. Owen is momentarily involved with the mud. I can't worry about the fact that his current stuffed animal favorite, a cat my mother's neighbor gave him at Thanksgiving, is going to be as muddy as he will be. It has momentarily eclipsed the previous inseparable, a cloth duck stuffed with batting another friend of my mother's made by stitching two pieces of a pattern together. He takes it everywhere, and its neck is now completely wrung of the batting. One day the head will separate from the body, and we will have to spirit it away, explaining to him that "baby duck," as he calls it, is "aouay."

His pronunciation is that of a deaf child, though his hearing is perfect. We have spoken about it to the pediatrician, who says we should wait and see; things may clear up on their own. Owen can't say "s" or lots of other sounds. First the duck was "baby dutt." We corrected him, pronouncing the *K* with emphasis. This he can reproduce; the thing that has already been more loved than the neighbor could have ever imagined, is now "baby duc-*K*." He noted one day that his hands were muddy: this he expressed as if a Swedish child learning English phonetically, "dirrrrr-ty 'ahnds." Now he has "dirrrrr-ty 'ahnds," as well as a runny nose. But if I am ever to get these assignments from my creative writing class read, it has to be now.

I have been reading in bits and pieces since yesterday, five minutes here, ten there. I lie on the sofa until attacked by small hands and a demand to read "Baaaaaahney Buch"—I speak to him in German, so what comes out of his mouth is an amalgam of two languages. This means a book about Barney the Purple Dinosaur, his newest discovery. "Baby DucK mit," is the way he says he wants to take the duck with him, mit-nehmen. Yesterday evening I made a fire in the family room and, while the alphabet ("ABC") song played over and over, my wife pushing the start button each time Owen demanded "ABT," I was briefly in the desert, in a stalled car, then in the diary of a run-on high school senior, whose motivation for wanting to bang one of two twins remained unclear, except for the usual reasons that boys want to bang girls, then in a world of earth spirits who spoke without contractions and met wind spirits who said things like "Great! Cool!" Now I dry off the chair with some of the leaves—I have raked leaves until my body ached from the strange contortions required of a rake, but something in me will not use the blower, the ultimate acknowledgement of suburban defeat—and sit. I am in the middle of a piece set in New Jersey, having finished a swoony evocation of darkness, the moon, and sex, and a piece whose cover is made from a paper bag with a little window cut in it and stapled back to reveal the title—very chic, I thought, and smiled, as at the pillow label used for decoration on the other notebook in the same folder: it's the same sensibility that leaves exposed brick walls and distressed wooden beams in multi-million-dollar museums of contemporary art, where huge sculptures larger than whales fill window-choked rooms that once housed mill wheels, or spun cotton cloth for a generation now long gone.

I have only read a page or two before Owen, bored with the mud, is demanding to ride in the baby's bucket swing. I try saying "No," my attention distracted from the stream-of-consciousness of New Jersey failure, ripped from my alternative worlds I have entered only in fragmentary bits and pieces for the last two days. I give up and get up, preserving some semblance of authority by insisting he take off the boots before I put him in the swing—it's just too difficult to get him in with them on, and they're on the wrong feet anyway, their frogs pointing slightly outwards rather than neatly in, as if as google-eyed as the frogs they mimic.

The sun is lower, and my hands are cold. I can feel the contrast between the warmth produced by my leather jacket and the line where the T-shirt begins. My knuckles are red; we will have to go in soon, and in any case Meg will be back soon with the baby, Teddy, "Bay-Tay" to Owen. This morning she went to her "Mom's group" (they're not mothers, they're "moms," as no real estate agent sells houses any more, but only "homes"), and I went to museums in Washington, a half-hour away from our house outside Annapolis, walking in the almost-winter sun of the National Mall up towards the African Art Museum, where a slow-witted docent poisoned the air of the exhibit called "Treasures" with her banal commentary to the works imprisoned in their airless Plexiglas cages and skewered under spotlights in the semi-darkness.

I had read the security checkpoints around the Capital were back; now they're gone again, and I was able to park without showing my Department of Defense ID to reassure the bored guard that I wasn't a threat and merely wanted, as I had done for more than 30 years, to look at pictures. Yes, I think, I am a civilian employee of the Department of Defense. One of the pieces I read later contained ironic dialogue by a midshipman at the Naval Academy—such as its author is, and all my students—meeting a girl in a bar. I think it's meant to be a meet-cute; she accuses him of learning the ways of Imperialism, and how to take over third-rate countries, as well as kill as many babies as possible. He escalates in what is apparently a joke, assuring her that the destruction of innocent civilians was precisely what they were being taught at Annapolis; to me it seemed difficult to believe the girl was getting his irony.

By now Owen has demanded to get "dowwwwwn." We have reinserted his feet in the green froggy boots—"me boot," he announces, "ja, deine Stiefel," I echo—and he has walked over some of the papers, making a smear that is probably mud but looks like shit. Perhaps the smear on the paper looks like shit because shit is such an integral part of our lives, erupting from two diapers and ending up on little boy clothing, my clothing, the changing pad, the rug, so that I have to run and get the rug cleaner, which leaves a stink of chemicals on my fingers.

The smear in any case—just mud in this case, I reassure myself—turns out to be not on the creative writing papers, but on print-outs for a trip I am taking in two weeks, a treat to my mother, who turned 80 this year. She called me this morning to nag me for the fifth time about a detail of the trip I had promised to take care of: she doesn't believe me, doesn't trust me, despite my being a competent adult, and doesn't know when to back off, though I told her after the second time she brought it up she had to stop bugging me. I got angry on the phone, then my wife at me for getting angry at my mother: "she's *80*,"my wife insists. I am caught with nowhere to hide. I made it clear to my mother weeks ago her nagging was driving me crazy; she doesn't understand and won't take on board that what she wants me to do only takes five minutes the day before through the miracle of computer and telephone, and that now I have had other things to do. Does she think I will do things faster the more they make clear they have no confidence in my ever doing them? Or is she simply unable to help herself? Dealing with my mother is only matched by dealing with Owen. He's constantly like a grenade with the pin pulled, ready to be thrown—sometimes he explodes, shrieking for an hour as if possessed. He wants his shoes, he doesn't want his shoes, he wants to go up, he wants to go down. The books all assure us he will grow out of it.

It's no use; I have to go indoors. It's too cold, and I can't concentrate.

Surprisingly, Owen accepts that it's "zu kalt," as I tell him. "Too kalt," he sort-of echoes me, and begins to pick up his things—the "meow-meow" now as spotted with mud as I'd feared, as is the box of raisins I'd let him take outside. We trudge inside. I think of making a fire, then realize the All-important Event, the Army-Navy Football Game, is undoubtedly over. Its results will be on Yahoo. I should check, if only to reaffirm my membership in my local version of the human race, and to break out of my alternation between the moment to moment intensity of food preparation, keeping Owen happy, keeping little behinds free of poop, and looking for the wire cutters so I can snip a wreath I'm putting up for Christmas so it fits around a too-large light fixture outside.

Navy has creamed Army.

My heart sinks. Then I rally. Did I want them to lose? That would only mean a victory for Army, sports being a zero-sum game. What one side wins, the other loses.

Still, I am not thrilled. Now they will be as full of themselves as the politicians who, having kissed the asses of the anti-gay-marriage contingent and lied about the war in Iraq, assert defiantly that their murderous foreign policy has been approved by "The American People."

After all, I know what it takes to get a winning football team. They sit in my classrooms, these overgrown, sweet, hopeless lunks, courted and ushered in the front door of a usually rigorous admissions process by the athletic department, beefed up for a year at the Naval Academy's Prep School, and dragged through courses for four years by the so-called Academic Center and endless EI, extra instruction, of people such as me. I do not think a winning football team is a good thing. It makes them think it's all worth it.

Yesterday I read a book review by Chris Hedges, author of a book I used last year with plebes called *What Every Person Should Know About War*. In this book, Hedges asks sober questions, and gives sober answers: what does it feel like to die? Will I keep up with my buddies from the field if I come home alive? What are the effects of war on a civilian populace? He makes clear that the adrenaline-rush of pumped up 20-year-olds firing rifles—he acknowledges the exhilaration of warfare, and says that those who engage in it feel like "killing gods"—is only the tip of the iceberg. What's underneath is that the whole fabric of life where the war takes place is destroyed for years to come: widows, orphans, maimed people: the few boys who come home in boxes are child's play compared to what we do to others. A fabric of life identical, save in the details, to my own this chilly December day. Yet many of the cars in Annapolis display magnetic "support the troops" "ribbons," cut-outs of plastic imbued with magnetic metal that enjoin us think only of the men wearing our country's uniform, not of all the other people dying daily.

And then I go back to the computer article about the football game, Owen momentarily distracted and the computer screen glowing in the half-light of the dark room. the Administration hawks whose offices are in the federal buildings behind where I parked my car today, those in fact laying waste to a far-off country and not joking about it like the character in the piece I read earlier, have used this event to intensify their power base, playing to their adoring fans, flipping a starting coin come from a devastated Iraqi city on the other side of the globe where men will no longer, and not for a long time to come, sit and sip over-sweet coffee on street corners, where houses are reduced to rubble, and where children die for lack of hospitals, or even the most elementary medicines. I am not pleased to see a sporting event turned into a political love-fest to support the authors of this kind of brutality, all of them people who will celebrate Christmas with their families in the warmth of home. The papers are full of the decorations of the White House. The First Lady has chosen white as her theme.

Now it is time to light the fire. I try, for a moment, to let Owen play alone to finish the page of creative writing that had been interrupted, but he is at least a few months too young, and I am thwarted in my attempt to find out what happens to my New Jersey stream-of-consciousness people.

Owen wants to crinkle the paper; he always does; it's his job. He sits before the fireplace throwing in the newspaper while I supervise. The ashes, stirred up, begin to sift through the air. We have to go plug in the outdoor Christmas tree, up uncharacteristically early. My wife will be back soon. I imagine the crowd, going wild in Philadelphia. How to argue with the sheer power of the blindness not only, it seems, of youth, but of politicians, perhaps men who want to wreak their will, or what they claim to believe the Will of God, on the world, the God who is invoked to help football teams win, and countries be destroyed.

I smile at my son, happily wadding paper before the cold fireplace, swept by love for the blindness of testosterone-fueled action, the necessity for encouraging him to feel the power that will one day be his and yet think of the consequences of his actions, realize that the world is a zero-sum game: if he gets to feel like a stud (as my students say) who controls the life and death of others, a killer angel (as Hedges puts it), those others will pay the price in daily misery.

At the same time, looking up at the couch with the half-finished pile of creative writing, I am swept as if a wave of warmth from a fire not yet laid with for the worlds evoked by other people I am entering in such distracted abandon, the worlds of a pile of paper, produced by people I think I know but, thank goodness, don't really—not really know, that is, so that they can still surprise me by bringing something to the table I haven't put there, like my son who is not a mirror of me but a separate human being, thank the Lord.

And this finally is what the written word does for us, as our children do, and the people like students whose presence, interactions, laughs and sulks warm our lives. It frees us from the imprisonment in our own world, detailed and intense though it may be, it is always our own—by allowing us, if only briefly and with distraction, to glimpse the flickering of a light that is not our own, seen as if far away in the night from a moving train between shit and ashes, and know, if only temporarily, that we are not alone.

But we get this warming realization only at the price of acknowledging ourselves only a cog in a vast machine. This requires a humility that those who crush the world under the heel of their boot do not, I believe, feel, caught as I believe them to be in the endless self-replicating hall of mirrors that shows them only themselves and means that anything outside must be implacably opposed. To acknowledge the freedom of others to be other than we are: this is the displacement of which those who see the world as an instrument for wreaking their own will are incapable, bathed as they are in the comforting feeling of their own body heat they imagine to come from the common sun, the whispers of their own voices echoed to the sound of what for them seems crowds. Courage! Conviction! Perseverance! Character! It's the cry of the self-satisfied, the masturbatory rant of those for whom the world outside is an extension of the self.

The fire has flared up, Owen sitting a decent distance away and watching, and now died down. Will the first log catch? Or will I have to put down my papers—I am half-lying on the couch again— and poke at it again? "Me turn," Owen will say—Owen wants to do everything, even dangerous things—and I will have to explain that no, it's Daddy's turn. And in any case, soon I will have to lay down my papers again and put the leftovers in the microwave, setting the table for two adults, two high chairs.

"Dinner tiiiime," Owen will announce gleefully. And we will echo, yes, dinner time.

Syzygy

A syzygy is an alignment of the stars: here the stars are aligned. I encourage young people to create personal worlds, knowing that they are part of a system that destroys such personal world, and read their results as part of my own personal world. I enter their personal world; I am in the midst of mine. Feeding the personal world of those I educate, or am the father to, could end in the circle turning back on itself, creating people who will destroy the delicate fabrics of such personal worlds. There is no way out.

The overarching question of this moment is perhaps: what is the relation of reflection to action? At least three layers are in alignment: I enter other people's personal worlds, an action which throws into relief my own; my little boys require nurturing as my students do and all of them grow up to be the men who play football and wage wars; though working for the Department of Defense, I go to Washington not for politics but to look at pictures, something made easier by my working for the military. And all is unified by the cold, the end of the day, the slight loneliness of a man alone outside with a small child (and another sleeping upstairs), trying to do his work in bits and pieces while baby-sitting, with both the politicians and the football players merging in the coin from Faluja, far away from where I am, further away from the "action" than even from the sidelines.

Ultimately the whole situation is a contrast of reflection vs. action much like Virginia Woolf's celebrated story/essay "The Mark on the Wall." In that piece, reflection is cast as female, (blind) action as male: but in this, all of us are male—me, my sons, my students, the football players, and almost all of the politicians. The particular elements of my world are, in a sense, irrelevant: each person has his or her own. What counts is their alignment.

Art

The aesthetic sense of life gives meaning to the flow of particulars through awareness of patterning. The problem that the aesthetic sense of life seeks to solve is therefore the same problem that the making of artworks seeks to solve, but the solutions—artwork on one hand, aesthetic sense of life on the other—are not identical. In fact, there are several problems with the solution of the artwork that the aesthetic sense of life escapes. First, that the artist's making the artwork presupposes interest at some further point that may or may not materialize. Second, that artworks become part of the same world as everything else once they are made; I return to these below. Still, the problem art seeks to address is he same that the aesthetic sense of life seeks to address, namely: the glut of particulars, data units, sheer details in the world.

Think of all the blades of grass in any lawn. Most people want only the sensation of "lawn," of a green carpet. But if we look closer, we see that there are worlds between every two blades, and three blades of grass in a row will make a symphony of near- but not absolute symmetries, little bending uprights that echo each other without being completely congruent, some leaning over others, a symphony of verdant scimitars. Paying attention to only one square foot of any normal lawn could take us a lifetime. Sane people, however, can't afford to spend their lives contemplating the blades of grass under their feet: we simply ignore the fact that the world is full of particulars, refusing to let it bother us.

Still, this unrecognized murmur of unperceived particulars is tapped over and over. It's the reservoir from which things we do notice surge.

For example, I notice the sudden April snow on the woods behind my house, which I see in the breaking daylight as I jump rope on the back deck. All the branches, not yet fleshed out with proper leaves but blurred in a green haze by buds, are outlined in a thin set of white lines, the snow not enough to accumulate but enough to accent. I see all the trees, the curvature of the ground, the trees that have fallen, with their roots up in the air like women in hoop skirts, roots meant to anchor the trees vertically to the ground but rendered non-functional by horizontality: the sun glimmers behind other houses, whitening the white, turning it all to a twisting complex of lines, filaments of lights and darks.

Yet it's only chance that had me up at that hour, chance that had me, or probably anyone, notice this. I can take the attitude that it's a good thing I was up. At least someone noticed it; somehow, it seems, this wasn't in vain on the part of the world. It almost seems as if I've saved the day, or at least the morning: I should be proud of myself, as I've been conscious of this virtuosity on the part of the world. I'm conscious of the "save": I got to see this after all. By the same token, the narrowness of the save—the fact that I'm not usually up at this hour at all—reminds me that most of the world goes unperceived. The fact of so much of what seems waste can remind me that little of it is saved in this sense—which ought to make me question whether the saving has a point, given that it's so rare. If I need to see the world to save it from non-being, that doesn't bode well for most of the world: after all, I'm not usually around. Indeed, nobody is, and somehow the world goes on producing these things, which may seem therefore wasted, like meals lovingly prepared that no one eats, that simply spoil and are thrown away.

The Russian Formalist theoretician Victor Shklovsky thought that a lot of the world spoiled in this sense and was thrown out. He was horrified, in his article "Art as Device," by a passage in Tolstoy's diary noting that when he, Tolstoy went to dust the table, he couldn't remember if he had or hadn't. Tolstoy is shaken with the existential feeling that the unnoticed is the unoccurred: we alone cause the world to have been, a later echo of Bishop Berkeley: *esse est percipi*, to be is to be perceived. Shklovsky echoes his feeling. The solution to this horrible situation, Shklovsky suggested, was to notice the world. He believed that it was only artists who made people notice the world. Hence his famous conclusion that "Art makes the stone stoney." Unnoticed, the world simply isn't. His conclusion is that art and artists are necessary for any of the world to be at all, to be saved from oblivion.

But Shklovsky was wrong about the middle term of his reasoning, the assertion that noticing only takes place in art. It can also take place in the aesthetic sense of life. I noticed the dusting of snow on my trees as the sun rose, and need never have tried to make art from this. Whether or not I try and transmit this perception to others is a subsequent decision that has nothing to do with the noticing, but we speak of art only if I do decide to make this attempt.

It's also a mistake to think that the world is producing finished meals that somehow are thrown away if we don't show up for them. In fact, it's only when we show up that there's a meal at all: our being there is what makes it a meal. This is so because what causes the noticing to happen is an effect not of the world itself but of what we, the perceiver, are familiar with. The reaction of interest we have comes from comparing what we're used to to what we see. The woods in the snow made an impression because it looked so different than it usually does. That's what we notice: a situation where we can establish commonality (same woods, same place) but also are aware of differences: how the trees looked in the snow vs. how they looked outside. For the same reason we think the world transfigured in the spring when, as in Washington as I write, the world is turned to frothing pink, with all the ornamental cherry trees all over the center of the city in gushing bloom. But if this were the norm, the way green leaves are, we'd presumably not notice them even if we saw them—or only the way we do the green leaves, occasionally, the sky dark, the air sweet-smelling, or in their first, pale green phase that itself looks so different from the norm. Green is no less startling a color than pink, only we're used to it. Interest is produced by variations from the norm: the fact that I have the background of woods without snow in comparison with woods with snow look interesting. Or the light of full day in comparison with which the faint glimmer of dawn is interesting.

There are other reasons why the world isn't spoiling if we don't notice it. It's true that all the things we liked, we noticed. However we tend to draw a false converse: if we could notice them all, we'd like them all. I fact, we'd simply be overwhelmed, which is why we fail to notice most things to begin with. It might be interesting, as an artwork, to take photographs of the same three blades of grass in my lawn over a period of time. But if we did this with the next three, and the next three, and the next three, people would turn away. The world can't be uniformly interesting; not only is interest the contrast of a tip with the rest of the normal iceberg, it's by definition a rare occurrence. We can't make all the world this interesting.

Nor is it somehow being unfair to the world that we don't notice a lot of it. Let's say we could get all the six billion people on the Earth busy noticing for every minute of their waking time. Or create another six billion whose job was merely to notice. Why would that be a better situation? Let's postulate all these people who are all busy noticing. The question then becomes: who notices that they notice? How does noticing change the world? Perhaps the world doesn't care to be noticed.

Why art?

Why in fact do some people feel the need to make art? Most people simply say to the person in front of them what they want to say: that's the form of their utterance. May I have the butter, please? Or: Don't take that, that's mine! Or: I love you. It's clear that such interaction is much more immediate than art, which involves taking a lot of time to make something of no clear immediate utility. This last is the eternal Achilles heel of art, the fact that we don't need it to fight wars, cure cancer, or put food on the table. The arts are the first things to be cut in school budgets, the first thing to be put on the national chopping block in moments of crisis: the crisis of the moment always comes first, or we're asked to wait until we momentarily have no crisis.

Artists need to begin by admitting a life-threatening crisis always has to be dealt with first, and that it's unlikely any specific artwork can help us with it. The time for art isn't when we have to repel an invader or fight cancer, it's when we don't have such adrenaline-pumping situations, when we can turn to things whose intersection with the world is less defined than the actions specific situations require. What characterizes artworks is precisely that their intersection with the world isn't well defined, certainly not by a specific situation that makes clear what we should do (repel the invader, get well).

Self-defeatingly, artists have typically insisted on fighting a losing battle with this one, by trying to deny that art almost certainly can't help us with a crisis. But why should it? In such situations, the only possible actions are very well defined indeed, and the hallmark of art is that its intersection with the world isn't very precise. Similarly, in most situations involving words, our verbal actions are very defined indeed; art casts a broader net, and lets people decide what its intersection with the world will be. If someone says, "Do you have the time?" we say what time it is, or explain that our watch is stopped, or at home. Our wiggle room is very small. But if artists could say what they wanted to say by opening their mouths and observing it to the person in front of them, presumably they'd do so: it's far easier than making artworks. Making artworks is to immediate communication as building a helicopter to fly us across the road is to crossing the street under our own steam.

So the question is, Why would anyone do this? Presumably, for two reasons, both of which must be simultaneously the case. First, that what the artist has to say isn't appropriate for immediate communication. Face-to-face communication tends to consist of things like "Nice day" on the trivial side, and "I don't love you" on the non-trivial. There's no place for something like Wittgenstein's "the world consists of everything that is so." To whom would one say something like this? Not one's mother, father, sister, brother, boss, or employee. So whom does that leave? It leaves the world in general: the piece of paper. Art, thus, requires having something to say that doesn't have an obvious outlet in the immediate world: we can't wait till next week and tell Cousin Alfie, for example. He won't understand it either. In fact, we probably don't know anyone who will understand it, or if we do, that's somehow not enough. Others—faceless, yet-to-be-defined others—have to be given the opportunity as well.

For, second, art is something that isn't complete until it's shared with others—only not any of the others around the artist, now or even perhaps later. Art must be externalized in the world where others can see it. Not, to be sure, specific others—thinking that artists are talking to the particular people who consume art is a common fallacy, produced by seeing the string of production from the wrong direction. Each person who (say) reads a book is a particular, but that doesn't mean that the book was written for particulars. That's why it has to be able to stand formally on its own: it simply sits there until someone falls over it or picks it up. The artist almost doesn't want to have too precise an idea of who that someone will be.

Why do this?

Why would people emit utterances at this level of postulated generality? Typically because there's no one to talk to about what they have to say, perhaps the fact that "the world consists of everything that is so." The other person might well say, "You don't say? One lump or two?"

The quintessential "going to New York to be an artist" young man is the sensitive one in a small town Midwest USA high school who is understood by no one but the art teacher (band directors in Midwestern high schools don't play the same role as the art teacher; they're part of the system that Doesn't Understand). Even so this much-told story works better if the young man, or sometimes young woman, wants to be something like an actor, rather than a painter—we don't quite know what painters do, but actors go to auditions. Being a performing artist is a somewhat shorter leash than the big-picture artists. And the story becomes that much more predictable if the young man in question thinks his sexuality isn't as standard as it might be: yet another reason to be Misunderstood, out of sync. You have things to say that nobody around you understands.

If you remain an artist once you get to New York, however, it's because what you have to say isn't something anyone there really understands either. If you simply find people like you, you flounder for a few years and then burn out before "getting a job." If you remain an audience it's because what you have to say isn't appropriate for your new immediate situation either.

Making art solves a particular problem for the artist: what to do with this thing that doesn't fit into the immediate world? Answer: put it where it belongs, in the sketchier world of "out there." For the artist, the particulars are airbrushed: effectively, it's a world without particulars. The artist isn't making works for specific others, with features, but for faceless others, the collective.

Problems with art

This means, necessarily, that what the artist has to say doesn't require a specific response; in this sense it's self-contained. Yet the action of making an artwork, something at this level of generality, only makes sense if in fact there is a faceless collective that could conceivably make contact with this utterance. This is a postulate of the artist. The problem is that only rarely does the postulate correspond with reality. But in any case this is beyond the artist's power; the artist is an artist insofar as s/he makes the postulate. The artist can't call this world into being. Its existence is an article of faith, nothing more. Perhaps there's no one out there at all.

If there's no one to say "Nice day" to, you don't say it. The lack of a situation means that precise things don't get called forth. Artworks get called forth anyway, but that's because they're not linked to precise situations. Artworks say things without the situation; the artist is the one whose action of making the artwork in a sense postulates the situation calling for it. It's like a response to a question that has yet to be formulated: the artist can "hear the question" in his or her head even if no one else can. If the artist didn't hear the question, s/he wouldn't produce the answer. But nobody else hears the question, so nobody will object if it isn't answered: if the artist makes the work, fine. If s/he doesn't, fine too—at least from the perspective of other people.

Artists emit utterances that are at a different gear setting than the one-on-one daily utterances of our, or their, everyday lives. By shifting it off the plane of the immediate, they open themselves to the fate of Chausabon in George Eliot's *Middlemarch*—who was engaged in a time-consuming waste of time that, at their death, is thrown out. Chausabon's life, presumably, didn't feel any different to him than the lives of those we later declare to have been unappreciated geniuses, and whose works are pored over after death. The fallacy of many artists is to assume that because they are working on things that do not intersect with the particular lives of people in the here and now, these objects will of necessity be hailed as artistic masterworks at some other time, with some other people. The fact that the audience is, in their imagination, faceless, doesn't mean it is so in reality: they still have to find individuals who will understand these utterances, even if these aren't the individuals around them.

It may be true that many, indeed most of those we now consider great artists in the post-Romantic world fall into this category of misunderstood in life, celebrated in death. But the converse is not true: that anyone who was unappreciated in his or her life will be such a great artist. Unappreciated is unappreciated: sure of your own direction is sure of your own direction. The further question, are you a genius or a failure? is not something the artist him- or herself can answer, or even determine.

It seems so logical to artists to imagine being appreciated after their deaths: all that has to happen is for someone to discover them. After all, all the writers we read were appreciated in this way. This is another case of a false converse. It's true that all the (say) books we read are books we appreciate. That doesn't mean that we read all the books that are, or that the fact of being a book suffices to be appreciated. Most writers die with their books in drawers, or if published, having disappeared without a trace, never having hand more than a handful of readers.

What artists gain by not demanding immediate reactions to their utterances is independence from the ebbs and flows of real-life taste: so what if the people around you don't understand you? It gives you some leeway for being something else than the particularly shaped person that will fit this specific set of circumstances. But you can't assume that the shape you assume will ever find a situation where it will be in sync with its world either: all you've done is save yourself now, in much the same way someone convinced that his or her actions will get him or her into heaven sees all that s/he does as part of living the life religion wants him or her to lead.

Ultimately, being an artist merely puts off the day of reckoning to some future date, as the religious person who asserts that his or her actions will too get him/her into heaven must at some point be proven right or wrong—s/he's just not able to come back and report to us. To the artist, it seems to change the nature of the justification, turning immediate into abstract. But it's only abstract because it's unknown. If artists could see how their works are received after their deaths—in most cases, not at all—they might think again about using this brave assurance that though they weren't appreciated right now, they'd (for that reason?) be appreciated in some future time. If the future is understood in a broad enough sense, there's never a day of reckoning: one can be discovered in 500 years.

The problem art was supposed to save us from hasn't gone away, it's merely that we've put off dealing with it. If your work is at any point noticed, it's not going to be by an abstract, but by particulars—somebody's Cousin Alfie, just not yours. That means you're waiting for another Cousin Alfie to come along: that's what justifies you making the work. You're forced to say that these people noticing your works has made them come to be, in much the same way Shklovsky thought that Tolstoy needed to know if he'd dusted for that to be, or the way someone in a lunatic asylum might think s/he had to go out and notice all the blades of grass in the lawn for the lawn to exist, or for that matter read all the books in the library to make their authors happy. If any of this mattered, authors would have to put off deciding if they existed by touting up from heaven not only the sales of books but also the degree of reader involvement. What if people read but saw something entirely different than what authors wanted them to see? Or saw but didn't perceive?

Writers might feel themselves becoming substantial in writers' heaven as someone reads their books down below—like Tinkerbelle brought back by audience members clapping to show their belief in fairies—and then fading out again as they realized that the person excitedly turning the pages of the otherwise long-forgotten book down below sees it as, say, an evocation of what, from that reader's perspective, was a bygone time. How quaint these people are! they're saying, as they turn the pages. And that hardly counts as finding an audience member who believes. All the other unread writers up in heaven are watching jealously, of course, and probably smirk with satisfaction as the author being read has to slink back to his or her cloud, realizing that though the reader is reading, s/he isn't "getting it" at all. No, this reader has not caused the writer to exist at all; better luck next time.

Boxes

A recent show of the works of Joseph Cornell suggested both the splendors and misery of going ever deeper into the caves of the imagination. A room in the exhibit in the National Museum of American Art in Washington was devoted to the shelves and shelves of "raw material"—pictures, objects—accumulated by Cornell in the house he lived in all his life in Brooklyn. What he made out of these fragments, his so-prim boxes with their fragmentary suggestions of more exotic lives—tropical birds, tinted prints of Renaissance paintings, evocations of hotels on the French Riviera—is simultaneously lush and cool, most of all evoking the person who made them, dreaming of an Outside accessible only in bits and pieces, evocative fragments, never as reality. Are they shameless wallowing in tourist-guide exoticism of the art deco era (the south of France is more interesting than Montana, it's clear)? Or are they wistful commentaries on the impossibility of ever achieving our desires? Perhaps both, and all of the above. They're both worldly, and utterly provincial.

Think of Cornell's house, full of this raw material, and also lined with the boxes and collages. In his mind, presumably, the boxes and collages were his reaching out to others; the raw material was what made this possible. But imagine living, a Cornell did, in a world where the contact was only postulated, not actualized, as it is when we walk through the exhibit. We ourselves have completed the electrical contact by coming to such an exhibition; we have added something that was only postulated before.

Because we only see the exhibits that are put on, read the books that are published and promoted, we may tend to turn into Dr. Panglosses of the artistic world: because we pay attention to these works, they clearly were the works that deserved to have us pay attention to them. A few minutes entering other artistic worlds—other countries' cultures, for example, or our own past that is full of now-forgotten names—should shake our confidence that what is had to be. In any case it's only a tenable position after the fact, when we can see what in fact is, to say that it had to be—in the same way that people opposed to abortion insist that the very people that are, are the people who had to be. This only works when we know who is.

What art is supposed to accomplish—making people independent of others—is actually not attained by art: artists end up being just as much at the mercy of others as anyone else, though in most cases past a point where they care. Perhaps this is the pay-off: they're not around to see, as Chausabon might have seen if he'd lived forever, his own failure.

Art works don't, moreover, transcend the world except in the mind of their creators. For others, artworks become their own particulars, the things out of which museums, and college courses, are made. They're embedded in their own worlds of particulars, and can be noticed or not to varying degrees and in varying relationships with their surroundings. They don't transcend the world, they merely become part of it.

Consider, for example, the way the works of art enter the landscape of the Hirshhorn Museum and the National Gallery East Building in Washington, and in fact fare rather badly compared to many of the objects around them in terms of interest and claim on our attention.

Water fountains

The water fountains in the still newish East Building of the National Gallery, Washington, are the dull-burnished moderne bronze bowls that have for many years been one of the highlights of a visit to the Hirshhorn Museum several buildings up and over the open area in the center of Washington known as the Mall. Here on the Mall, people make moving patterns across the grass of Frisbee games, wear paths that at some point require snow fencing (regular in its dull red slats and irregular in the fact that it cannot be kept perfectly upright and at a right-angle to the ground and so sags in irregular tilting patterns), and move along the white gravel of the paths or sit in the inadequate shadows of the trees when the summer sun grows hot, the repetitive oom-pah-pah of the carousel before the Victorian gardens behind the Smithsonian Administrative Building, called the Castle for its American redstone Gothic hodge-podge of turrets, arches, and rondels.

These fountains are the highlight of a visit to either museum, irregularly-arranged glistening half-globes arranged over the so-perfect circular form, silvered against the gold color of the background as the face descends closer to them, forced for an instant to enter into their world as if pressing the eyeball up against a *trompe l'oeil* box or a sugar Easter Egg with a pop-up scene inside of bunny rabbits, chicks, and flowers visible only from one side. They contrast with the formless dark-marble basins of the older National Gallery building, great baby bathtubs that continue down from the marble on the wall and that are so large and strangely curved far outside the contours of the face that they seem alien, somehow a part of the dark-wood and marble bathrooms for the elimination of bodily waste a bit further down the corridor rather than the visually refreshing baths of these smaller curved shells into which the face dips in search of splashing water, cool against the tongue.

The Hirshhorn fountains are the highlight of the downstairs; the upstairs levels are another delight, the sun shining dully off the marble
floors and intersecting with the white square pedestals topped with
Plexiglas cubes in which shimmer individual works, moving away from
the viewer's eye in a diminishing curve, casting a right-angled forest of
shadows and catching the sun on their shimmering side, curving out of
sight around the edge of the circle of glass asymmetrically looping
around the fountain down and in the circular courtyard within, rising and
falling with the reiterative weight of the water, slightly off of all centers,
the fountain off-center in its basin, the basin off-center in the ring of
glass, the ring of glass off-center in the shell of the building, stable and
unstable, punctuated with the huge shadowed green ears of wild tropical
plants casting cut-out shadows like dark-struck Matisses across the floor.

The glistening water droplets do not stay put in the discs of the fountains; each spurt onto the tongue loses at least half the stream down onto
the metal, which causes cataracts among the existing droplets, spattering
upwards to join with others and cause rivulets that draw them down-
wards to the drain like the rain rivulets down the sides of hillsides cutting
through the otherwise newly greening patches. There is a constant re-
arranging, a constant consolidation as a drop loosens its grip and begins
to slide, joining with the other drops in its way and for an instant leaving
a trail that in a moment separates into new droplets like a solid line turning into dashes and then dots.

And then there are the galleries. In the National Gallery, remembered
landscapes of paint strokes are evoked by brief glimpses of paintings
against white walls, people in singles or pairs before them, entering or
leaving doorways: the feathery near-pastel strokes of the eyes on
Tiepolo's "Madonna of the Goldfinch," the pudgy set of the Child's
mouth; the burnished curves of hand and shoulder in David's "Napoleon
I"; the strangely small cluster in the left side of Georgione's "Adoration
of the Shepherds," with the golden glow of Joseph's beard; the dot of
white standing for a shine on the lip of Vermeer's "Girl in a Red Hat";
the haunting shadow-play below the cheekbones, all turned to a mess of
faint darkenings, of Leonardo's "Ginevra da Benci." All of these details
are arranged on their mental shelves waiting only to be drawn out by the
slightest far-away tug at that part of the brain, knowing that getting
closer is useless, as it will only find the same things it has already found
and filed under the place allocated to that arrangement of color and tex-
ture, a confirmation rather than a discovery.

And in the garden courtyards, the stone cupidon strangling a goose
while water gushes from its throat and makes dark patterns down its side,
the ever-changing and ever-constant splash of the gurgle meshing with

the cold curves of the white stone benches, the plants reaching up to the glass ceiling, the murmur of voices changing, ever the same and ever altering.

Storehouse of particulars

The world is a vast storehouse of particulars seen only to ourselves, refusing to stay still long enough to be referred to save in the collective, tiny fragile jewels like insects that flit by us and then immolate in the unseen air. How to hold on to the pattern of the droplets on the fountain bowl? The gushing of the water lapping from the throat of the stone goose and staining cupid's gray forearm, making his fingers glisten?

In order to determine whether the works of art have been really and truly seen, we can't merely take a tally of visitor numbers. Yet for publishers or museum boards, that's the only number that matters—how many books are sold, whether or not they're read, how many "bums in seats" are in theaters, whatever the people attached to the bums thought or perceived. One woman peers at a metal plaque at the door and says, "Room 12. We've been here before", though this is the room with the maze of shadows under the cheekbones, or if she prefers, the only Leonardo in North America? I am too familiar with these works, they too unfamiliar. What, anyhow, would be gained if I could grab one of these blind tourists by the elbow and bring them to the face of the Child in the Tiepolo, the strange feathery tree in the Monet under which the girl whose face is caught in shadow reads, the serpentine removal of paint in the Fragonard "Young Girl Reading" where the artist reversed his brush and drew a curling line to denote lace with the wooden part of his brush, lo these centuries ago, room upon room of the movements of brushes bearing color to reveal themselves to the close-up eye?

Things become even more problematic if I remember that even I am not getting so much from these paintings this time around. Nor can I necessarily congratulate myself on being a better perceiver of these things than the people who make a quick swing of the gallery room, as if to confirm that they do in fact contain paintings (for such people the preferred method is to keep their eyes at the level of the title, to be told that this is *really by Rembrandt*, and then glance up for a moment to see that there is actually a painting hanging above). After all, I remind myself that I once put down *Madame Bovary* in perplexity.

"Getting something" from artworks, in short, is a problematic undertaking, sporadic at best, moving in quirky ways. Besides, if someone could make a list of what we were supposed to "get" from an artwork and test us to see if we had, the result would be the dead "teaching of classics" that happens in all too many colleges and universities—not a sign of the life of the artworks, but of their death.

The processing of artworks, like the rest of the world, can't be reduced to formulae, no matter how much college Deans, and Professors, would like to do this. Artworks solve no problems intrinsically; they only create more. All of these problems are the raw material of the aesthetic sense of life.

Chapter Three
Public Rhythms

WHEN WE ARE SIMPLY INGESTING THE WORLD we can approach it with the aesthetic sense, allow it to form its own patterns and be aware of them. At such times we are not under pressure from outside forces, not being screamed at or tugged at by other people, not preoccupied with everyday worries. Our bellies are probably not too empty, our bank accounts not too depleted, our children not in danger, and the people who matter to us not in imminent danger from invaders.

Such times, however, are fairly limited. Both of the examples I offered above involved some degree of solitude: in the case of the museum, almost absolute, in which people were far away; in the case of the winter afternoon outside, the solitude of an adult with a small child. But most of the time, we're not alone. Proust shows us what we have to do to ensure that we have this meditative float for more of our lives rather than less: never marry, keep romantic entanglements of whatever sort to a minimum, have enough money, let someone else do the housework, and have no job in the usual sense. And of course, no children.

In such a world we can afford to be aware of all the delicate variations on the rhythm of life, exercise the aesthetic sense of life in unimpeded fashion. This becomes more difficult the more firmly we are locked within the social world. For this reason most people can exercise the aesthetic sense only within worlds defined as not their own: we don't know how things are going to play out, we're at least to some degree on vacation, and with fewer firm commitments.

Indeed, what makes our "own world"—in the geographic sense of our own world—our own—not worlds outside—is that we have a sense of fore-ordained structure, the way things are going to be. Leading a social life means doing things that are to a much greater degree not within our personal sphere of influence, and not unknown to us, as it feels in worlds outside our own. Life here at home has markers that show us the passing miles, to which we look forward and which we remember with pleasure or regret: days, weeks, week-ends, annual holidays, life-transitions, the passage of time marked out in a series of milestones small and large, so that in passing each we sense we have achieved something, done something worthwhile with our lives.

These are the public markers, what most of us rely on rather than allowing our lives to offer us their own structures—this last the definition of the aesthetic sense of life. So these public markers—ubiquitous, and so determinative for most of us—are an alternative to the aesthetic sense of life. They're the way everybody else, the collective "they," wants us to structure our lives. In fact, they're the way most people do structure their lives.

It's possible to be aware of these and still not be overwhelmed by them: we see them, acknowledge their power, but still don't necessarily give in to that power. The aesthetic sense of life can continue under the patterns they mark out. Problems begin when we take them too seriously: it's Friday, so we have to be looking forward to the week-end. What if we're not? It's Christmas, so we should be merry. What if we feel glum, precisely because we're supposed to be feeling merry? It's Valentine's Day: Oh no! We forgot to buy chocolates! Such public structures don't leave a lot of wiggle room for personal likes and dislikes. They require constant sacrifice to the gods of rhythm: we have to do these things whether we want to or not.

If we become too dependent on these for meaning in our lives, we are left high and dry if suddenly we find ourselves suddenly situated at a level above them from which they simply seem not to matter: they were never ours to begin with; what if we cease buying into them? For many of us, the truly dangerous times are those when we abruptly find ourselves suspended above the milestones as if having an out-of-body experience, our perception drifting in the air as we look with curiosity at the discarded shell of ourselves, far below, inexplicably toiling towards yet another goal that will be achieved and passed by in its turn. We see these mountains that normally would present such challenges to us, that we spend our life in scaling and descending from far above: we are no longer beholden to them, but by the same token they no longer mark our progress. The elaborate interlocking mechanism of wheels of which we are composed as gone into neutral, the teeth no longer interlocking, the wheels turning but with no purchase, so that they whirr and whirl.

The aesthetic sense of life protects us from becoming too firmly wedded to any one set of markers, and saves us from panic when they are absent: it allows us merely to let life continue, confident that if we pay attention to it, patterns we had not thought of will emerge. The aesthetic sense of life gives us a way to understand the public as themselves malleable, changing, so that we can use them to pattern our lives without seeing their control as too absolute. We can be aware, in the same gently smiling way, of the power these rhythms have over us: we can allow that power to hold sway, but being aware that it's happening. If we find a way around that power, we can take it without feeling that we are contravening the fundamental structure of the universe.

Too great belief in public rhythms marks both foci that adjoin the aesthetic sense of life: the too specific, and the not-specific enough. All churches develop rituals, which they justify as saying that the Almighty wants things this way. All of the very worldly develop rituals too, which they justify by saying simply that this is the way things have to be. To look at public rhythms from the aesthetic point of view means to ask how strong their power is rather than assume it, be willing to accept changes when these occur and perhaps initiate them when we want to, and to be alive to the ongoing *comédie* of their birth and death pangs.

Métro, boulot, dodo

Métro, boulot, dodo, say the French, to note the rhythm many in the West allow their lives to beat to. Life can be summarized by the eternal rhythm of getting to work on the subway, the *métropolitain* (*métro* for short); you do your work (slang: *boulot*), then you go to sleep (*dodo*, the child's word for taking a nap). And then you get up the next day and do it over again, and over again, and over again—until one day you don't. Or, more probably, until one day you're out for a while, back in for a while, out for a longer while, and then finally you cease trying to keep up the rhythm and let it slip from your fingers.

Métro, boulot, dodo: it seems so much more reiterated than the Anglophone equivalent of the same idea, trochaic trimeter, each foot rhyming with the next. The closest thing in English is probably "the old rat-race" or "the daily grind." These expressions lack a sense of alternation, being much more unrelenting and un-punctuated by change than the three-step French version, not to mention more fraught with unrelenting competition and pain. The French version is clearly more urban as well, perhaps a reflection of the overwhelming presence of Paris in the French mind.

German too conceives of the rhythm of modern life in terms of animals, though not rodents. In German, it's horses who mark the time; we speak of the *Alltagstrott*, the everyday trotting along. It's more passive in a sense: the horse isn't going somewhere, not even on a racecourse or in a cycle. It's just going.

Santa Monatinga

This greater periodicity of the French version of the human condition, not to mention perhaps its feeling of being less competitive than the Anglophone, may come from vestiges of France's Catholic, rural heritage, shining faintly but unmistakably through the modern overlay of urban life involving the *métropolitain* and *boulot* rather than the yearly rituals of reaping and harvesting.

In Medieval days, in France as elsewhere in Catholic Europe, the day was punctuated by the rhythmic offices of the Church, the weeks by the approaching feast days of saints and the religions calendar, and each person's life by a handful of recognized offices of the Church, like boxes waiting to be checked off: baptism, confirmation, marriage, and finally, extreme unction. A French friend of mine, perhaps presaging the disaster of his marriage, remarked to me on the day of his wedding, in front of the village church ringing out the approaching ceremony: "The next time these ring for me, it'll be for my death." Church bells mark the signposts of a lifetime.

Nowadays most of us, especially in America, catch only faint glimpses of these built-in ecclesiastical rhythms to the day, year, and lifetime. There are some, if only we can hear them, as in the children's song "Frère Jacques," enjoining a monk whose ecclesiastical title of *Frère* (Brother) has to be mis-pronounced with two syllables, Frayr-eh (his name, the monosyllabic Jacques, also turns into two beats) to stop sleeping (*dormez vous*—are you *asleep*???) and ring (*sonner*) the bells for prayers. "Sonnez les matins," it ends, before the final "ding-dang-dong" of the bells. "Matins," the early morning prayer for monks (and by extension for the most pious lay people), is rendered nearly unintelligible by being stretched out to three syllables. Still, Jacques is supposed, even in the twenty-first century, to get cracking with the regular bells and prayers, the marks of the day that make it carry on.

The echo of a long-lost daily routine is faint in this song; indeed many of us learn its French as if it were only gibberish. My wife grew up hearing her mother sing "Santa Monatinga" for "sonnez les ma-teen-uh." In the same way, jokes abound about children thinking of the great patriot Richard Stands ("to the Republic for Richard Stands") in the Pledge of Allegiance. We have other hints too, buried if already deeply in our Western cultural memory, of this world of people whose days were punctuated by the bells. The sticky-sentimental picture of peasants bowing their heads at dusk in the fields by the nineteenth-century painter Millet, called "The Angelus" (they're listening to the sound of the church bells), hung in many homes in the West until well into the twentieth century. Perhaps nowadays it is only the Islamic world, with its several-times-a-day prayers that still builds rhythm into the day in this fashion, that religious observances punctuate the day. Men unroll their prayer mats in airports, in the street, in the corner of stores, at the appointed time to pray to Mecca, oblivious to the particulars of their surroundings, fulfilling the destiny of the rhythm for acknowledging the Almighty. (It's too indecorous for women to put their behinds in the air in public.)

It may be only religion that has enough sway to cause us to stop what we are doing and, literally or metaphorically, unroll our prayer-mat. This is surely what gives pathos to the plaintive cry of T. S. Eliot's narrator Prufrock in "The Love Song of J. Alfred Prufrock"—if someone named "Prufrock" really is the narrator of this strangely disembodied lament so drenched in frustration and nostalgia: "we have measured out our life in coffee spoons." The problem is presumably not that life is measured out, but that it's measured out in such trivial markers, the accoutrements of polite, and utterly meaningless, chit-chat. Lacking religion, as we assume Prufrock does, all that's left for him are the empty rituals of social interaction. Not even measured out by cups of coffee, which at least tastes good and gives a sort of sustenance, but by the thing used to stir it that you can't even drink: things can hardly get more formulaic, or emptier, than that.

TGIF

There is a sense of unrelenting blur implied in the notion of a "rat-race" or the *Alltagstrott*. But we too avoid the sense of blur by paying attention, as Jacques was meant to do with matins, to the things that measure out our lives in things other than coffee spoons. The things that break up the *Alltagstrott* for us are quite different than the religious rituals within months, weeks, and days that regulated the world of the Middle Ages. We have, for example, our week-ends. Thank Goodness It's Friday, we say; TGIF. There's even a chain of mall restaurants called TGIF, whose decor, and whose menu, seem to be touting the virtues of easy sloppiness associated with the now-useless objects of the past. All nooks and crannies of the restaurants are filled with prefab "old" things; the servers wear a hip version of barbershop quartet suspenders and striped shirts with many picture-buttons that makes them seem almost clown-like, as if it were really a circus; the food is all comfort food, rich sauces, pasta, and overflowing plates. It's Friday: kick back and relax.

There are smaller sub-divisions within work days as well. People look forward to lunch, and then again to five o'clock. At the beginning of Hitchcock's *Psycho*, we see an undifferentiated landscape of anonymous buildings. The titles inform us that this is "Phoenix, Arizona"—which we associate, at most, with hot, and then that it's "Friday, Dec. 11, 2:43

p.m." We're meant to be puzzled: Friday means something to us, but 2:43 p.m. is neither lunch nor quitting time. And in fact, it turns out the couple in the building the camera's all-seeing eye enters turns out to be taking an illicit and by now grossly extended lunchtime for sex. Hitchcock knows it's not a time that punctuates our life, that this is a betwixt and between situation: illicit goings-on (the woman quickly becomes a thief) in an imprecise time.

Most of the same people too who so look forward to quitting time, or to Friday (the restaurant is sometimes called merely "Friday's," as if the mere day of the week were sufficiently laden with positive connotations to allow it to stand alone as a name) have larger caesuras in their lives as well. The upper-middle classes in the United States take their winter break in Florida, and their summer vacation avoiding sunburn at the seashore or avoiding the mosquitoes in Maine.

These sorts of punctuations, large and small, rustle underneath the more publicly-determined ones of holidays. In the annual scale, for Westerners, and increasingly the world that trades with it, Christmas is the most complex ritual, the most drawn-out, and the most demanding of public recognition. People sometimes talk of going away to avoid Christmas, but it's not clear there's any place untouched by the Christmas curse. Some protesters limit themselves to rolling their eyes at the fact that the local mall thinks it's already Christmas well before Halloween: now we pass directly from Labor Day, which has meaning only as the end of summer, to Christmas.

A Visit from St. Nicholas

Public markers of the passage of time, such as Christmas (as we now do Christmas) may seem absolute for any given time, but in fact they are always in a state of transition. They accrete: the traditions now won't be the same as Christmas a hundred, two hundred, or even fifty years ago. That's the way public markers develop: everybody adds something, and some additions stick, altering the nature of the thing itself.

The twin icons of Christmas American-style in the twenty-first century are the tree and Santa Claus. Neither is particularly religious, though they have a small religious core. In this, they serve as an example of the way the quiet accretion of detail that gradually creates public traditions, like layers of mother of pearl on a grain of sand. The metamorphosis of the Christmas tree from Martin Luther's symbolism for eternal life (the fir tree remained green in winter) to the Victorian import (Victoria's husband was German) to the stuff of the local department store is such a case in point. Who now thinks of the symbolism of the tree? Who reflects on how bizarre it is to have a cut tree in one's suburban house! Someone seeing things from the aesthetic point of view might.

It's easier to do so the week after New Year's in a city, when the sidewalks are piled high with, of all things, dessicating *trees* now, horizontal and waiting for the trash, so clearly so far from home. They didn't seem so bizarre coming in, as they did so in stages, and were full of sap and life. When they're thrown out, by contrast, it's all at once; they're dead, and they lie about on the curbs.

As for Santa Claus, most people are aware that the Americanized version (fat, red pants with a red white-trimmed tunic, boots) dates only from the illustrations to the early nineteenth century poem "A Visit From Saint Nicholas," more popularly known as "'Twas the Night Before Christmas," usually ascribed to Clement Clark Moore and dated 1823 (a rival claim exists that dates the poem's composition twenty years before and gives it to another author). Even this has developed. The poem itself, which suggested that Santa arrived in a sleigh and came down the chimney (in Europe he comes early in December, arrives at the door, and leaves candy on twigs for good children), had the good Saint (the historical prototype of Saint Nicholas has survived in name only) as miniature, as are his reindeer—as he'd have to be to come down a chimney. The illustrations that gave us a vision of Saint Nick erased the notion of his being an "elf" or small, so we're left with the irreconcilable conflict between Santa's girth and the bore of a chimney—indeed, a normally slim person can't fit down a chimney—like those equally irreconcilable conflicts that dot Shakespeare's plays, say whether Othello's pretty-boy ensign Cassio is married or not.

Now we've added Rudolph to the eight reindeer of the sleigh, just as we've added Frosty the strangely metaphysical Snowman—who comes to life because of a hat and wants to play hard because he knows he's melting away and has to move fast before he's water—not to mention a host of other accretions, as valid or invalid as any other accretion to the germ of a religious belief.

Sometimes the attempt is made to resist the most recent of these accretive changes; no one bothers with the ones a layer or two back, much less even deeper ones. Now Christmas is simply about shops and buying things; the strength of merchandising in our world is simply too great to be withstood. Those who want Christmas to be something else are fighting a losing, or rather lost, battle. "Put Christ back in Christmas," we hear. Conservative Christian groups demanded vocally that public figures' Christmas cards in fact be Christmas, rather than merely "Holiday," cards, and wish the receiver "Merry Christmas" rather than merely "Happy Holidays." This is one of those miniscule changes the soldiers in our culture wars set such store by, and that end up mattering so little. The greeting on a card? No one is suggesting boycotting department stores that do too much Christmas, arguably more noxious to the notion of religious worship than a few words on a card.

Religion as public structure

One of the potentially most viable sources of public structure is, therefore, religion. Religion is so absolute in its claims, however, that integrating multiple religions, multiple structures, can be problematic. The more they are, the more inevitable it is that they will rub off each others' edges. Individually, they are bound to accrete, becoming wrapped in layers so think we can barely see the humble beginning of the great snowball of tradition buried deep within. Krishna, the much-revered avatar of Vishnu, has associated with him many stories that owe nothing to any sort of Holy Writ. Much time is spent evoking for example the story of the baby Krishna, Hinduism's answer to the Baby Jesus, stealing butter or honey and being punished either by his mother or the bees: such scenes are the stuff of many dances in the South Indian dance form Bharata Natyam. If Santa and Christmas trees in malls are invalid, so too is the story of Krishna as a butter thief, or the countless statues of him as a toe-sucking baby.

All religions accrete in this way. We may make fun of what we call cargo cults in tropical coastal areas, where visits years before by religious figures from outside implanted a few practices kept alive and changed like the message in the child's game of "Telephone" so that when, decades later, a cargo boat arrives, it finds the indigenous people practicing rituals that bear only the most tenuous connection to anything recognized as authentic. Yet all our religions are in this sense cargo cults. It took a while for Hinduism to decide that the Buddha, otherwise the most prominent figure in a rival religion, was in fact one of the avatars of Vishnu as well. And most all gods in Hinduism turn out to be aspects of others, and all of the Brahma, simultaneously one of the primary trinity and that into which it is subsumed.

So too for Christianity. The same French friend who mused on the way church bells would mark the steps of his life shook his head the first time he saw Saint Peter's in Rome: *Je ne sais pas ce que c'est*, he said, *mais ce n'est pas une eglise.* "I don't know what it is, but it's not a church." Who among the church fathers, or the followers of the Middle Eastern prophet whose life and teachings inspired their religion, would have dreamed of the splendor of Renaissance or Baroque Catholicism? And reactions against all this—the Lutheran Protestant Reformation, or even stricter sects: Methodism, wearing black, disapproving of cards and dancing; or the Quakers with their lack of service and unadorned meeting-houses—are merely reactions against excess; they don't approach the original. And who says approaching the original is the thing to do? That's to deny the passage of time that is the nature of our human existence.

All the dogma of dogmatic religions, as well as the laissez-faire attitude of the non-dogmatic ones (the Unitarian-Universalist Church calls itself "a church without a dogma") has been developed over time; in most cases we forget the reasons for practices and have to be constantly reminded of them, if anyone even knows. In any case they're different than what people did a mere hundred years ago, not to mention centuries or millennia.

Palimpsests

But it's not just religion that evolves more and more layers. All life is in this sense accretive, everything we do a palimpsest—as literary theory of the 1980s insisted rather tiresomely was the case with written works, as if this set them aside from the rest of our existence. (A palimpsest is a Medieval manuscript on vellum, sheepskin, whose first text, scraped away to allow re-use, still showed through the later one in ghostly form: we get this in paintings sometimes too, where an artist has gone back to eliminate a minor figure, re-arrange an arm, change the small dog in the crook of Milady's arm to a bouquet of flowers.

Language too is a process of using words in unaccustomed ways. Sometimes, for a time, the ghosts of earlier usages hover behind what we say. In this case we're aware of using "poetic speech" or metaphors. But this is the exception rather than the rule. If we speak "sharply" to someone, is this the same "sharp" as scissors? A metaphoric use? Or a literal use to mean this particular tone of voice? Is there a literal word? "Harsh"? Is this borrowed from something else? We don't know; that's just what we say. And using technical vocabulary—let's say we could describe a "sharp" tone of voice in terms of timbre or oscillations of sound waves—isn't any more literal, as we can use these same terms to describe other things.

Some terms do seem in the process of losing earlier meanings; some in a kind of historic limbo where a few initiates know but most people do not. Even when we speak of the "rat-race," it's unlikely anyone but a poet think of rats. We go jogging nowadays in our cushioned running shoes; only the most dedicated scholars of the language realize that "jogging," was once a term, like "trot," applied exclusively to horses. For us it simply *is* running without sprinting.

Slang is language of a sub-group that has literal meaning to those in the sub-group but a kind of palimpsest meaning to those outside: teen slang is always evolving, and always sounds quaint to outsiders. Something is "cool" (not literally frigid) or "bad" (means "good"): to those on the inside, it's unlikely that these will seem at all odd.

Yet most of language is a corruption of earlier language: the French *chaise longue*, long chair, has become the say-it-without-blushing "chase lounge" of the Anglophone world; an Anglophone "curfew" started life as a French *couvre-feu*, the hour at which the fires were to be covered. Yet it's doubtful that even a Frenchman would think of fire as he said this. Linguistics studies things like vowel-shifts: how over time one set of vowels routinely became another. The changes are so endemic to what we do we can't hold them still long enough to single them out. It's like pointing out the obvious fact that our bodies are made from the bodies of millions of people before us. We usually don't like to think of this, preferring instead to see ourselves as ends in ourselves, or the products at most of a few countable people, our parents and a generation or two back.

When something like Christmas takes on the dimensions it has—and beyond, overshadowing much of the rest of the year—it diminishes the importance of many other less important public holidays. In the West, indeed, summer is seen as the big romp, and then there is Christmas at the other end of the cycle. The importance of most other holidays has receded to allow Christmas its unchecked spread in the public realm, the sole structure larger than Friday, the end of the work week, that has meaning to most people.

Wheels within wheels

All of these cycles when seen from the aesthetic point of view resemble the pre- Copernican vision of the heavens: wheels within wheels, as if we were all condemned to the fate that awaits Charlie Chaplain when he gets caught up in the gears of the vast machine in *Modern Times*. Chaplain is chewed up by the gears and spit out; we spin with the various gyres of planetary motion, some small (the dramatic curve rising to lunch and falling to time-to-leave), some mid-level (where so we go this year for spring break?) and some large (will we make it to our 50th wedding anniversary? do we have enough money for retirement?). All of it produces the music if not of the spheres, then the residual background hum that is the result of the simultaneous spinning of all these cycles of which our life consists.

We don't see them this way, most of the time, because to us it looks as if we are coming up to the next completed cycle. We're not caught in the gears, the gears are internal. Our point of view is from within, not from the outside. It's only the outside that sees a cunning inter-connection of planets and orbits, as one of those models of the heavens that a child can set spinning with a turn of a handle as a dance of hoops. From within, what we see is the slope up to the next high point; what we sense is the ascent or descent within the closest series of peaks. We never see it all from an airplane.

Seeing from without

Or hardly ever. Sometimes poets horrify us by removing so com-pletely from our point of view we are left gasping, as if having the wind knocked out of us: all we see is the mess of cycles and gears that sud-denly seem alien. We don't know what the point of it all is, seen from the outside. It's only from within that it seems to make sense, because from there it's our anniversary, our graduation, our wedding. Many readers of Thomas Hardy feel the wind knocked out of them by his sudden jumps between vivid evocation of who said what and what things tasted like on one hand, and the simple flick of his hand that wipes away this so-vivid world when he seems to lose interest and note that, after all, everyone here is long gone: the voices that one instant ago were so loud and bois-terous echo in abandoned chambers as if having been simply neutralized by a powerful sweep of the arm of time.

As, for example, at the end of "The Three Strangers," one of the *Wessex Tales*, Hardy evokes all too well the taste of mead made from high-quality honey, the agitation of the housewife that the price of her daughter's christening party is getting out of hand so that she constantly enjoins the teen-aged fiddler and the serpent player to play only so long (too much dancing makes too large appetites), the deep basso sound of a singer's voice. And then, as if having abruptly lost interest in the world he created, Hardy gives a gesture of impatience in his too-abrupt closing:

> The grass has long been green on the graves of Shepherd Fennel and his frugal wife; the guests who made up the christening party have mainly followed their entertainers to the tomb; the baby in whose honour they all had met is a matron in the sere and yellow leaf. But the arrival of the three strangers at the shepherd's that night, and the details connected therewith, is a story as well known as ever in the country about Higher Crowstairs.

It's as if the rug had been pulled out from under us and we thud to the ground, or rather as if the ground itself had simply been removed so that all we held solid no longer is and we feel ourselves falling with no support into darkness. All these are dead: it's the "oh well, no matter" flick of his pen that re-consigns it all to the darkness of death if not forgetfulness, shown by the end of the story. "The paths of glory," as Thomas Gray memorably put it, "lead but to the grave." Or any other path, Hardy adds, it seems somewhat sourly.

Such "well, we all die so nothing matters" wipings-away of all human striving seem brutal. Faced with Hardy, we feel like children that some loved adult has seemed to truly care about, involving him- or herself in our sports, our dolls, our trucks. Then abruptly s/he turns away, dismisses us with a flick of the hand: we were nothing but filler for an idle moment. What we thought was real interest was only pretense, or perhaps an atavistic impulse that was played out sincerely, but quickly exhausted itself.

Ghosts

To be sure, we're fascinated by the possibility that what we do is meaningless, the tantalizing realization that there is a great world outside the whirring gears of our own desires. Escaping the wheel of desire is, after all, the goal of Buddhism; it's not achieved by many. Most of us are content to be titillated by the prospect: we shiver deliciously at the thought of ghosts, spirits of the dead. What if they haunt us? The notion of creatures just beyond our ken seems fascinating to us.

It shouldn't. For reflect: Whom do the ghosts have to be their own ghosts? We're scared of the dark, but for the creatures of the dark that is home. We are fascinated by the notion of living on past our deaths, simply because we're not sure we can. But we're not at all interested in the notion of being alive in five minutes, because we assume we will be. We need the boundaries in place to think transcending them interesting. what makes the ghosts shiver? The pathos of Anne Rice's vampires is surely that they themselves do not have a world of the undead one layer beyond them to provide a foil to their own existence: it's a boring existence, in a metaphysical sense.

Take sexual desire, a world in which we're caught by our own desires if there ever was one. Socrates is asked, in the early pages of Plato's *Republic*, if he's sorry he's of an advanced age where sexual desire has begun to lose its hold on him. Not at all, he says; it was a cruel mistress, he's glad now to have escaped its goad, riding him as it did. For Shakespeare, lust was like a "bait laid on purpose to make the taker made"—as if we were drawn forward by a hook imbedded deep in our insides, and a string protruding from our mouths. Lust is so absolute a need that we take great pains to allow its satisfaction for a limited time—in the young—and then strict rules about keeping it within bounds thereafter. If allowed to slop over its banks, nothing, it seems, would withstand its force. We have to build dikes. It's considered bad form, almost disgusting, if the aged make fools of themselves for lust, but fairly normal for the young to do so.

Sexual desire certainly binds us to a set of wheels, setting goals we aim to achieve. Would we really want to be free of their power over us? To us caught within the wheels it seems all too comprehensible: we're hot for so-and-so, and not for the other so-and-so. More generally, we're hot for (say) girls of a certain type. Of course. But that's only because we're caught within the gears. Think of the way we look on dispassionately at the mating of other animals: we're unable to say what a starfish finds attractive about another starfish, a horse about a horse. We suspect stallions don't even make distinctions between (say) one mare and another, so long as she gives out the mating smell.

But male/female is something we can process. Think of the imaginary aliens that have populated our imagination. In a beguiling movie by Nicholas Roeg called "The Man Who Fell to Earth," with David Bowie, the loving couple of aliens make love by oozing liquid all over each other from their fingertips. Of course, they're human actors, so these aliens have to be divided into male/female (typically, inserter/inseminator vs. inserted/eggproducer); but imagine aliens even more alien than these. Our movies generally give all aliens heads and eyes and arms and legs, very few make them look like amoebas. But let's imagine they are, and that (like the mythical creatures of Plato's explanation for homosexuality) they have more than two sexes, and hence many variations of coupling; let's imagine they don't insert or allow themselves to be inserted into. We'd quickly lose interest.

Which doesn't stop us sometimes from wishing we weren't so possessed by lust. Even at times like this, however, we're most interested by an unattainable world just on the other side of our own, not by things even further away, or things we can in fact attain. We wouldn't like actually to be as removed from the draw of our own sexuality as we are from the sexuality of even horses, much less the sexuality (at what point does the word become inoperable?) of aliens without heads, limbs, or insertable members. Let's say they "have sex" by sniffing the air. That's uninteresting.

Let's say we're tantalized by the thought of regaining our own youth: if we were back in our once-again-young bodies, would it be with a memory of ever having been old? If not, how would that be different from the first time around? Perhaps we have already been whatever age we are in our bodies. If we do remember, we can't, in that sense, be young again: we would look every morning in wonder in the mirror at our suddenly unspotted hands, our suddenly unlined faces.

Disengaging ourselves from our own cycles—really disengaging—is as strange, and as scary, and abrupt, as it is to see Thomas Hardy wipe away as if suddenly bored the sights and sounds on which he has lavished so much time and care. We sense this strange lack of impulsion forward only a handful of times in our lives, if that often. And for most of us that is enough, or more than enough.

The music ceases

Perhaps we sense this abrupt cessation of the music of the spheres after the death of a loved one. Perhaps it's a gulf we fall in when, having lived on for years by ourselves in a house our children tried to get us to sell, we finally trip and break our frail bones. From now on out, we suddenly know all too clearly, our time will measured not even in coffee spoons but in days in a hospital bed, perhaps a brief Indian summer in a nursing home, repeated visits to a hospital, and ultimately will end. If we are conscious of this inevitability, here we may well despair: finally we've run out of wiggle room. The vast machinery of our existence stills for an instant as we see it whole. It is not a pretty sight.

Such splits in the earth to reveal the depths of molten metal within— or, in Dante's version, the ice at the center of Hell—are not something we can usually survive unchanged. Yet some of us have forced upon us more frequent, less serious, less apocalyptic, and more bearable senses of this detachment from being chained to the wheel of life. Perhaps they come upon us as often as a time or two every year, or every few months, where it seems we float above the surface of the Earth, momentarily liberated of the necessity to push our feet against the hard surface of things to propel ourselves forward.

At such times, the music of these spheres is gone as abruptly as if a wire had been detached, or as if we had gone momentarily deaf. The cessation of this noise so much a part of our life we are unaware of it until abruptly it is gone almost hurts our ears, like turning off the jets of a Jacuzzi bathtub in which we've drifted for so long our skin is pruny to abrupt something-beyond-silence, the silence underlying silence.

In such a world without one of its constituent aspects, things seem to drift: No longer anchored to a cycle or a crystalline sphere containing their orbit, they unroll in front of our eyes incapable of predicting the next frame of the movie like a cheesy vaudeville scroll of passing countryside unrolled and re-rolled behind a cut-out car in which two people pretend to walk.

At every sensation we think "Really?" "How odd!" We are strangers in a strange land. Everything is, if not marvelous, at least amazing. Not the least amazing thing is our sense, as if aware of being a character in our own dream, that we're amazed not because the things themselves are out of the ordinary and hence worthy of amazement, but merely because they lack any tie to the rest of the world. Each one comes to us as a surprise.

These are the moments the aesthetic sense can protect us from: most of life will seem to lack structure. But the aesthetic sense knows that it is only a matter of time before a structure begins to emerge, like a body rising from the weeds to the surface of the pond. The aesthetic sense can't say when the body will emerge, and its faith that it will is only faith: perhaps we will die before an overall structure emerges. But at some point something will happen, and the aesthetic sense allows us to be ready to be aware of it when this happens. The aesthetic sense is a sort of waiting wakefulness, interested to see what the world has to offer.

Langue/parole

What is the point of achieving this structure? This may well be the most fundamental question associated with the aesthetic sense of life. The linguistic philosopher Ferdinand de Saussure develops the distinction between *parole*, what an individual emits, and *langue*, the generally shared system of these sounds that can be used to communicate with others. (The distinction is expressed in French, even when Saussure is translated into English, because English lacks this distinction between individual and collective language.) Sounds only achieve meaning if others understand them; only the shared can be used to express or create human warmth. *Parole* isn't, to be sure, nothing: the individual can make what sounds s/he will, it's just that no one else will know what to make of them. Nor is *parole* powerless; gradually many people doing things their own way, assuming this way is common, changes langue—but only slowly, and in a collective way. The collective isn't, in any moral sense, better than the individual, it's just that only the collective has meaning.

Similarly, the myriad of individual details of which our lives are composed have no meaning for the collective: they're just there. The details of my life are interchangeable with those of anyone else: the specifics of Owen's froggy boots, the smear on the paper, the New Jersey sex piece, the cold air and the oncoming night—*mutatis mutandis*, these are identical to the details of others' lives. The point for the aesthetic sense isn't the particular nature of the details, only that they're there, serving as the body that is structured. For it's only configurations of these details that have meaning—which is, necessarily, meaning for others. And in identifying these configurations we're suddenly able to talk with others, offer them something that they too can understand. What others can understand and share with us are patterns, not particulars. These are like the things they see in their own lives, or are possible for them. Particulars separate us; generals unite.

The distinction between *parole* and *langue* isn't absolute, in that many examples of *parole* can alter *langue*, and if the *parole* follows the rules of *langue*, the two are separable only conceptually, not in practice. (If I say something comprehensible to others it's both *parole* and *langue*; it's only if my *parole* diverges from *langue* that the two can be separated in practice.) The structure that is the material of the aesthetic sense isn't separable from the particulars it structures: the particulars create their structure. We respect the particulars of our lives by letting them create their own meaning, letting the chips fall where they will and then seeing if there is a pattern. But what we get from the aesthetic sense is a sense of structured particulars, just as *langue* and *parole* fuse when meaning is created.

This explains how, in reading or perceiving, we can be struck by individual details—in the body of *langue* we can see *parole*. But individual details alone are meaningless, just as we may live a whole day that seems pointless: we have eaten, drunk, and slept, and all to no point.

Consciousness of pattern is the aesthetic sense of life—patterned particulars. The pattern justifies the particulars, because the pattern is *langue*, the particulars only *parole*. We know that if there were another person present, s/he would understand it—and in fact there may be another person. But we need not actually share it with the other person, any more than if we are following the rules of *langue*, we need another person to be there to hear us. It suffices to know that if there *were* another person, s/he would understand.

In this, the aesthetic sense of life has the advantage over making artworks. The production of art involves the postulation of real others, at some point and under some circumstances. The aesthetic sense of life is merely consciousness of the structure: it postulates others as really existing, but does not postulate a particular event in the future—for art, the perception of the artwork by other people. Making art on a desert island where no rescue is possible is senseless. Finding meaning through the aesthetic sense of life under those circumstances, by contrast, makes perfect sense.

The worldly, those who live only in their particulars, condemn themselves to loneliness: no one else cares about their particulars. The truly religious, those who trade in all particulars for another meaning visible only to them, may well achieve meaning: God never changes. But this meaning is at the price of all particulars—for most of us, too high a price. Only the aesthetic sense lies in the middle, acknowledging the particularity of our lives and the presence of other people.

Chapter Four
The Aesthetic Sense Outside

THE AESTHETIC SENSE OF LIFE MEANS, we go about our business, whatever that is, and see what, if any, patterns life makes. We're part of life, in which we act, but are conscious that it's bigger than we are. Because we must adopt this "squinting" perspective that simultaneously lives life and is conscious of its patterns, we're aware of the aesthetic sense most strongly when we are in an unfamiliar place. Of course we're marginal in such places: we're supposed to be; they aren't our world. We're not "on vacation," which becomes its own rat-race of looking for specific experiences X and Y; we're just in a place that's not ours, looking to see what we see, whatever that is.

For me, as for most Westerners, two such places are Egypt and India. In what for us is the world outside foreground and background are reversed with respect to the world inside. In the world inside, the details of our life are given, and the patterning brings them to the fore. In the world outside, the details are already at the fore, and the pattern merely arranges them. In the inside world we take details of the world for granted and become aware of the structure that gives them retroactive value; in the outside world we take nothing for granted, so that what comes subsequently is the structuring. In the world outside, we're aware of everything. The problem thus is not that we take everything for granted, but that we take nothing for granted.

These are examples of what it's like to see the world outside with the aesthetic sense, letting meaning emerge.

In the Brief Egyptian Spring

Visitors from the West to Egypt, such as me, are always invoking, and evoking, the past. Seated on his horse before the pyramids, Napoleon—whose rediscovery of Egypt led to the decoding of hieroglyphics by Champollion and altered forever the world's understanding of the Pharaohs—addressed his troops: Soldiers! From these monuments, forty centuries of history watch you! The soldiers, according to stories, then went on to show their lack of reverence for the historic weight of the monuments; the Sphinx, still at the time half-covered by sand and crouching at the foot of the pyramids, was used for target practice. Or was that their revenge on the past, their attempt to whittle down its massive weight to something like manageable size? It's the same past that Western visitors two centuries further on come to see, perhaps thereby rendering it human in scale rather than merely awe-inspiring.

Egypt has entered the Western consciousness as a place passed over by history whose long receding moan has left it high and dry—from the City of the Dead in Cairo, the necropolis of sultans and of commoners (where countless thousands of more recent Cairenes live and procreate among the building-like graves; the tombstones make convenient tables), to the royal tombs at Luxor and the Valley of the Kings, to the disinterred relics of those kings in the Egyptian Museum, to the crumbling mosques of once-powerful rulers who were hung from the city gate when the next wave of invaders arrived, to the no-longer-cosmopolitan city of Alexandria built on Greco-Roman ruins.

Perhaps it is right that Egypt, for the outsider, is drenched in loss and melancholy. Contemporary Egypt, I come to realize during my time in the brief Egyptian spring, is a country on economic life support. Its population doubles every terrifyingly few years, the United States pays its bills (Egypt receives the second-highest sum of US foreign aid; Israel receives the most), and it produces no products the outside world seems to want except a venue for tourism for its pre-Islamic splendors. Only recently, many years after its disastrous mid-and late twentieth century wars, has it achieved a modicum of stability and something like prosperity for the newly empowered Egyptian upper-middle classes. But these scratch and claw to maintain their foothold. It's a country where a state of emergency has been in force for almost 30 years, where the (increasingly powerful) fundamentalist Muslim Brotherhood is outlawed and its members routinely arrested, yet also one where women without veils are increasingly harassed, and where the president-for-it-seems-life now apparently wishes to groom his son to take over at his death.

A tiny minority of Egyptians escape to the international level with degrees from the University of Chicago or the London School of Economics; the vast majority still walk behind oxen in the fields made fertile by the Nile. Typically they dream of going to the city—which, should they ever make it there, will swallow them in its slums. Despite the substantial squarish space Egypt takes up on the globe or map, its arable (and livable) part is miniscule, under 3% of the total area of the country: the rest is desert. Aside from the nomads, its population, almost equal to

Germany's, crams into a string-like riverine country shaped like a papyrus blossom at the Nile's delta on the Mediterranean with its stem of Nile banks reaching upriver to Upper Egypt. Its cities are stacked north to south along the river: Alexandria, Cairo, Luxor, and Aswan, with development over in the Sinai in the form of tourist hotels along the water's edge. Increasing wealth, however, means increasing building and "development" on this tiny area of arable land. Which is why the Americans have to feed the country.

Rising expectations

If foreigners feel melancholy, it seems that what Egyptians feel is frustration. One recent novel set in a real building along one of Cairo's main streets, Alaa Al Aswany's*The Yacoubian Building* (technically it's too indebted to Mahfouz's "cluster of people in the same place" structure perfected in books such as *Miramar* to be too interesting) makes clear the price in money and influence of living space in downtown Cairo, and the even greater price of scarce places in the national schools that can lead to a steady job and a middle-class existence. Rent control means people stay forever in apartments, and find ways to give them to their children: the pressure of people wanting to move in has no place to go but to grind people ever closer together. In this world, people pay ridiculous bribes to be allowed a maid's room on the roof. To be able to eke out any sort of life, you have to know somebody, your father has to have the right job and status, and then you have to go ten times to every office to get someone's signature only to be told again and again to come back tomorrow. A television series of this book is planned for Egyptian television, I read in *Egypt Today*, though the outrageously profligate gay character is being changed into a straight one in the television version.

A sociologist named Galal Amin whose books are published by the American University in Cairo Press has developed a theory of "the frustration of rising expectations" to explain the rising tensions of Egypt today. Before the Nasser revolution of 1952, suggests Amin, the foreigners and the aristocrats ran everything, and so people had no expectations to be frustrated. With the Egyptianization of the country and the elimination of the monarchy, it seems to the people they should have a chance, when in fact they don't: there are simply too many people for that. The winnowing of winners from so many more losers takes place through nepotism, the exchange of money, and influence-peddling. Realizing this leads to frustration, and that, according to this professor, to the rise in Muslim Fundamentalism, a profoundly middle-class (rather than peasant) movement.

The mechanics of society for the average Egyptian are, Amin suggests, time-consuming and spirit-crushing. The huge Stalinistic block-building called the Mugamma (a gift from then-Big Brother USSR) that towers over Cairo's main Al-Tahrir Square, catty-corner to the Egyptian Museum, is according to reports a nightmare of Kafkaesque bureaucracy. An article in the *Christian Science Monitor* (by Sarah Gouch) notes: "For many, the 56-year-old Mugamma—built to offer people one-stop shopping for birth and death certificates, passports, visas, and more—is a nightmare to be avoided. In the comic film, 'Terrorism and Kebab,' the Mugamma's bureaucracy so frustrates the lead that he mistakenly grabs a guard's gun, is labeled a terrorist, and proceeds to take the building hostage."

I get a slight whiff of this frustration at the equally imposing main train station, the Ramses Station, through the process of changing a train ticket. If such a minor operation is so cumbersome, I can only imagine what more substantial encounters with paper-pushers must be like. The train station is imposingly "Egyptian" in style, though its façade is pointed toward what seems a spaghetti of flyovers, small shops, street vendors, and impassible alleys rather than toward the open space it deserves, and perhaps at one point had. In the middle between the two uncloseable public entrances is a huge and imposing wooden doorway as if for a cathedral or mosque, closed: this is the Royal Entrance, opened only for the King (and now, the President). I am amused by the notion of having to have a special door: this shows respect, I think, a concept whose importance to me in the fabric of life here becomes ever clearer during my time in Egypt.

I have had the hotel purchase a ticket for one (me), round-trip, on the fast train to Alexandria: the tickets for the two separate parts of the journey simply appeared at the concierge's desk in an envelope, looking like miniature college diplomas written in Arabic, complete with seal. On one the concierge helpfully wrote "To" and on the other "From"—there is otherwise nothing that I can read on them. But now, it turns out, I need tickets not for one, but for two. Ahmed, friend of a friend whom I met the last time I was in Cairo—27 years ago—who is my guide and companion for much of this trip, was horrified at the notion that I would go to Alexandria alone: he is coming too, he insists. This means changing my single for two together. Impossible to do it by phone, and the concierge of the hotel can't have it done: it's just too complex, he says. We have to make our way across town and do it ourselves. And so, a twenty-minute cab ride over the Nile later, I accompany Ahmed over the piles of mismatched shoes and the food vendors on the sidewalk across to the train station in our quest to turn one such perfect little diploma ticket pair into two.

First Ahmed leads me to a ticket booth far off the main concourse. He speaks with the man behind the glass for far longer than I'd think necessary, then turns, clutching my tickets. He explains that the tickets can be turned in and exchanged for two together (we are going down a class, as Ahmed refuses to travel first class), but only if we get the signature of another man in another office, pay more money, and accept losing an exchange fee. Ahmed leads the way into the station proper; a few sweepers in turbans are all that, at a quick glance, differentiate it from a faded French provincial station. We find the other office, tucked away behind some ancillary tracks. A man at a paper-strewn desk looks up; there follows more verbal back and forth. Many minutes later flourishing signatures are appended to pieces of tan paper torn off of note pads, stamped with a rubber stamp bam-bam, and handed over.

We return to the first window. The bam-bam papers are produced, and the old tickets. More voluble talk. It's not clear to me that this is going to work, but finally it does. We have the tickets! In only an hour, much traffic, much palaver, and two offices later, the tickets are changed. We are going to Alexandria, where history tells us Alexander the Great's body was returned for burial; no one knows where.

Alex

Because I am a foreigner, I cannot—it seems—avoid the pervasive suck of melancholy that configures outsiders' reactions to Egypt. The past is even more insistent to such as me in Alexandria than in Cairo—Alex, as locals call it, when they're not Arabizing it into Al-Iskandria, which strikes the visitor as a French city gone to seed, like Algiers, or a larger version of the Portuguese fantasy of Goa, now almost completely Indianized across the ocean. The city of Cleopatra and Anthony—or for that matter of St. Athanasius (of the Athanasian Creed) and the old Library of Alexandria, themselves more than two millennia beyond the pyramids, midway between us and the things the tourists come to see—rises to the surface only in stuttered scars across the mottled surface of the neo-European constructions, or (more recently) are being hauled up from the depths of the Mediterranean, covered with barnacles.

The sub-title of a recent book on Alexandria, by Michael Haag, is "City of Memory"—itself a phrase penned by Lawrence Durrell, the Western writer most identified, at least by Westerners, with Alexandria. All attempts to convince foreigners they should visit Alexandria quote effusively from the so-called *Alexandria Quartet*, four rather windy romans-fleuve (that, *pace* the implications of this collective title, have

nothing to do with music) by Durrell, an expatriate Britisher who lived
first in Cairo, and then the Alexandria of World War II, and then evoked
the Mediterranean city in fictionalized memory from a Greek island well
after the fact of his residence there. His works set in Alexandria are
meditations on what we know and don't know, versions of the same
story with the same revolving and somewhat tiresome set of largely
European characters stranded in this peripheral but still clearly Mediterranean city: the woman his narrator loved, Justine; the British diplomat
Mountolive; the lesbian painter Clea who's in love with Justine; and the
poet loosely based on the Greek poet Constantine Cavafy, Balthazar.

Durrell's prose, for anyone nowadays who tries to read it seriously,
seems overwrought and, as the Germans say, *schwülstig*, as overheated
and sticky as the waiting air just before a thunderstorm. Yet he does at
least mention places that still exist. In the Cecil Hotel, we're told, the
fictional Justine awaited. In the bordello quarter she sought her daughter.
In this street so and so... Durrell tries hard—too hard—to evoke a city of
labyrinthine intrigue, of European decadence set here on the fringes of
the Mediterranean civilization, its people living out their marginalized
lives as self-conscious second acts.

I stayed across the square from the faux-Moorish Cecil, new at the
time of Durrell and now a member of the French Sofitel chain, in the
Metropole, a place whose finery has been cleaned and pressed but not
fundamentally saved from ruin—whose hugely high French windows
with their views of the tram stop, a huge hand-painted billboard, and the
violent Mediterranean rattled in the wind at night, and whose lobby contained a third-rate oil picture of perhaps Queen Elizabeth I and Walter
Raleigh, so dry the canvas was missing in flakes. When I arrived, a
greeter in a natty suit arrived with a lemon squash on a silver plate.
Downstairs in the corner of the building is the celebrated patisserie Tri-
anon, with its dark wood art nouveau curves around inset mirrors giving
back what until later in the day is a deserted shop, its glass cases full of
trays of sweets for children for the Prophet's Birthday. In front of the
Metropole the palm trees are mature and seem to bend without being
threatened by the ferocious winds from the sea into which people lean as
if in danger of being carried off: up on the Eastern Harbor, at the end of
the Corniche, the palm trees are younger, and permanently disfigured by
the wind, protected by sleeves of banana leaf thatch that keeps them at
least more alive than dead.

Guide books to Alexandria for Westerner tourists (there aren't many
these days) lean heavily on Durrell, but also try to make what they can of
the poet Cavafy (1863-1933). Cavafy—whose name was anglicized from
Cavafis (as he's still called here) when his father emigrated to, and for a

time lived in, England—left a book's worth of poems about beautiful young men who died young, used up by sexual excess, and about the glorious lost past of the Greco-Roman Alexandria, by Cavafy's time completely paved over for the European city. His fame, intense in some poetic circles, was largely posthumous. The guidebooks encourage the visitor to endure his flat-turned-into-a-museum (the turning having happened half a century after his death), decked out rather forlornly with scraps of writer's memorabilia (he wrote at this very desk!) and the ghostly plaster death mask of a lumpy, ugly old man. It's in a nondescript building in an unprepossessing alley. A plaque at street level directs the visitor upwards: here lived Cavafis.

A hundred years ago in this city, one reflects, Cavafis/Cavafy was already making poetry about the melancholy of decadence and the fog of memory, his beautiful but doomed young men in one poem living (and dying) in the early twentieth century, in the next in the second century BC, in the next in the world of Anthony's conquest—all these echoes of vanished worlds and their pathos acting like organ chords to enrich the quotidian reality of the moment, evocative in its very ordinary sordidness.

Initially, I read, Cavafy had the same reaction to Alexandria, and dreamed of leaving. That proving impossible, he made the best of a bad situation. And now Cavafy's melancholy spector has itself added to the melancholy of the city that has continued on beyond him. *This* must have been the view he saw from his window, a guidebook notes under a photo of unexceptionable buildings over our heads as we walk down the alley, and shows a street like any other that the individual sensibility even a century ago had to work its magic upon to make it even worth remarking. Now it's worth remarking, it seems, because Cavafy can be assumed to have remarked it, the contemporary visitor taking interest from his or her interest in someone who once, long ago, was interested in it because it was his world. This is memory built on memory, loss built on loss.

It's odd, this city whose claim to Greco-Roman fame is that so little of this city remains (the largest chunk is a Roman theater and its complex by the train station, recently excavated by Polish archeologists). And how important is it, really, to be told that E. M. Forster, at the age of 38, had his first homosexual tryst with a tram conductor on the Ramleh line (whose terminus was outside my hotel by the billboard)? This event is chewed over for many pages of Haag's *Alexandria: City of Memory.* "City of Western self-centeredness" seems more like it. No wonder a recent memoir by André Aciman of growing up in, and subsequently leaving, Alexandria is called *Out of Egypt*, in echo of Karen Blixen's *Out of Africa*, about white people in black Africa, a time and a place recalled from far away. Both titles ooze loss—Africa, whether white or black, is a place one leaves, and writes about after. As, I suppose, here.

Tobacco

Sometimes the nostalgia is quite self-conscious. Three pictures now hang in a column up the wall by my bureau in suburban Washington: they are advertisements for Egyptian cigarettes from the early decades of the twentieth century, cleverly framed with off-white mats coordinated to their colors—one beige, one brown, and one slightly green, framed in gold-on-red frames that pick up the glistening gold of their images.

The pictures themselves are small masterpieces of lurid design. Two are for cigarette brands with Greek names, in one case Cairo, in the other Cairo and Alexandra. The third is Alexandria, but a French name: Carvellis Frères, with a guarantee of the quality of the cigarettes in English on the top, an assurance that comes out upside down when framed: perhaps this one was the covering for the box, so that this would have ended up on the bottom.

All the Greeks, as well as the Armenians and Jews, who gave Alexandria such a polyglot flavor and provided much of the business in Cairo, were exiled in the 1952 Revolution or shortly thereafter, in the Suez standoff of 1956—in many cases leaving homes and businesses as they were in their haste to board boats to other, safer, Mediterranean cities only a Greek or Italian island away. Their moldering villas in Alexandria have been abandoned by the sea, or, set on the dusty and increasingly ugly side streets of Cairo, been turned into banks.

The images in all three of the cigarette pictures—how surprised the printer would have been to see what were the transitory advertisements or box coverings for perishable objects that went up in smoke framed so cleverly and lovingly; surprised perhaps as well that these pictures had made it safely from Cairo to Vienna in my hand luggage, and then to Washington—are amusingly "orientalist," even for the time in which they are made. They are self-conscious kitsch to sell a product for which kitsch was the international language (think of our own "Dutch Masters" cigar boxes, our cigar-store Indians). In one image, a sultan hugs the knees of a (fully-clothed) odalisque who obviously holds him in her thrall; Cleopatra-type fans stand behind them. The Carvellis one includes images of pyramids, Anubis (the god of the underworld), and the Sphinx tipped in shiny gold paint; the third, the Alexandrine Greek, Alex Livanos, is a misty desert scene—palm trees, a Bedouin on a camel, the lone and level sands stretching far away.

I bought these in an antiques shop in Cairo called *Nostalgie*, its name parading its own self-conscious self-regarding—not just an antiques shop, it seems, but an antiques shop about the act of buying antiques. No further deconstruction necessary. *Nostalgie* is in Zamalek, a once-ritzy section of Cairo where now, on its main drag, an entrance ramp to one of the Nile bridges shadows the shops at anywhere from ground level to several floors up. The shop was small but not overloaded, not dusty, and well-lit. The other things for sale were pictures of the freedom leader Saad Zagloul, plates, some less interesting pictures, and dishes.

"Antiques" in Egypt, I had learned, are generally a mixture of over-heated French copies and Ottoman excess, all of them children and stepchildren of Istanbul's Dolmabahçe Palace, itself Europeanizing gone mad with a Waterford chandelier touted as the largest in Europe (and it *is* still Europe, by about 100 feet of land beginning outside this reception room and ending at the water that divides the grass from the Asian side of Istanbul) and a "crystal staircase." On this, the metal posts holding up the banister are encased in sleeves of sparkling glass as if having survived an ice storm. All the mirrors are edged with golden curlicues, all the picture frames worked in mother-of-pearl—emblematic of the rest of the palace: excess for its own sake, an orgy of "more is more." These more typical Egyptian antiques shops are dirty and spilling out with junk, an amalgam of French and Ottoman, pushed to ferocious complexity— life-sized dark metal statues holding lamps in need of glass shades, tables ornamented beyond anything approaching decorum—shabby, scuffed and tattered, the picked-over relics of the foreigners who fled, abandoning treasures picked up for a song by the rising Egyptian bureaucratic bourgeoisie, or come to rest in these holding places for unwanted things.

Never have I seen so many simpering niads holding fingers to bronze lips as in the dusty back rooms of shops just off what had been the main square in Alexandria, the center of the European City in an urban agglomeration where the Arab city had grown exponentially outwards, south into the Nile delta, and where yuppies were in the frenzied process of erecting and buying high-rise condominiums miles away along the Corniche, up by the Montaza Palace and an unfinished Four Seasons hotel, where the Mediterranean crashes dramatically against the rocks, raising huge curtains of spray. Never have I seen so many forlorn pictures with their paint chipping as in these Alexandria antique shops, their frames separating, never so many dusty pressed-glass bowls, never so many pieces of "French" furniture, almost all the worse for wear, the shabbiness of an overwhelmingly shabby city: Alex, abandoned by its cosmopolitan world, pumped up with money from the Egyptian merchant class uninterested in these relics of a lost world.

Most of the buildings too in Egypt are scuffed, many are decrepit. By my hotel back in Cairo, I walk past relics of the British that, mutatis mutandis, could have come from Bombay or Calcutta: "Pyramid House" is my favorite, in art deco from the 1930s, though it's nowhere near the pyramids, washing hanging from its balconies with their view of the stagnant Nile below, echoing the equally sluggish Tiber in Rome. The building façades are spotted with age and falling plaster. All in all, however, this form of aging is far more aesthetic than the active rottenness of a Calcutta. This is a dry heat after all; things corrode more slowly, or degenerate by flaking off rather than growing mold and turning rancid. The cars puff huge clouds of dark white smoke; the gasoline, I am told, is still leaded. This must take its toll on the buildings too. I have read that Cairene policemen have the highest levels of lead in their blood of any group of people in the world.

Zamalek

Nostalgie, unlike these sadder, messier antiques stores, was a proper shop, mentioned in a guide to help expats acclimate to Cairo, head and shoulders not only above the junk shops in Alexandria but also the newer versions elsewhere in Cairo, in the tourist areas. Worst of all these was Mahfouz's "Palace Walk," now chock-a-block with holes-in-the-wall selling the same repetitive boxes, glass perfume bottles, and the identical King Tut replicas, and manned by men scanning the clothing, conversations, and reactions of passing tourists for clues which would tell them which of a half dozen European languages to offer their wares in. "How may I take your money?" they ask, their faces searching yours for a clue to your nationality. "Willkommen, benvenida, que vorrete comprare? Entrez!"

Nostalgie was on a quiet street of Zamalek, the area dotted with embassies (Tunisia, Malaysia). It was up the street and around the corner from the long-entrenched Gezira Sporting Club, on whose dusty horse track I went running in the mornings, before I discovered that it was more fun to run along the sidewalks above the Nile, saluting and saying "Good Morning" to all the sleepy guards with AK-47s lounging in their chairs as the sun rose on the restaurant boats lined up along its shore. The track was overflown (if that's the right word) by the approach (fly-over in British English) to another one of the Nile bridges, one bridge south of the one emerging from Zamalek to span the river. I ran under the roadway seeming to hover above like a huge bird of prey, by a groundskeeper's little house with piles of pots tucked into the shadow. In the shadow of the highway, the dirt track that exhaled puffs of gray under my feet dwindled to a single lane, went around a broken fence, and made me wonder how anyone, man or horse, could run on it properly.

Many neighborhoods in Cairo had these surreal fly-overs to Nile bridges apparently planned well after the buildings and leaving whole worlds in their shadows that were usually used as car parks, or in some cases were only tortuous pedestrian mazes involving illegal cross-overs, tiny islands between two directions of chaotic traffic, and fences not meant to be traversed, requiring crossing traffic with no light (you hold out your hand at the rushing cars, as if this alone would dissuade them) up to the end of an illegal island, and then making your way along the curb down to another place where you can cross, taking your life in your outstretched hand.

The Gezira Sporting Club was a time warp of its own, I learned, with its height-of-chic-in-1955 leatherette chairs in a no-atmosphere club-house building embalmed by the smugness of its own exclusivitity. Nonetheless there was a croquet lawn, a small putting green, and places to sit outside under the palm trees—all of it offering a less expansive feeling than the comparable club in Bombay, where the sheer emptiness of the playing fields were what made the layout so surreal, an island of tranquility off the teeming, pullulating streets. But in Cairo the streets do not pullulate with people, beggars are minimal, and the river is nearby with its balustrades like dusty unkempt versions of Roman walkways along the river, flowing along considerably lower down, to offer open space. Trees do not, by and large, grow from the roofs of seemingly abandoned buildings in Cairo, as they do in Bombay or Calcutta: instead an ugly gray concrete slab building will have been shoved in on one side of a decrepit villa, and another on the other side; an arcade once meant to mimic the Rue de Rivoli will have been cut off after only an arch or two to allow taller, uglier buildings to intrude. It's not a ruin, as Calcutta seems to the Westerner, it's a world inhabited by people who don't seem to get the point, or with other things on their mind.

Tourists

Up the road from *Nostalgie* is the Cairo branch of the French shop Fauchon, in Paris behind the Madelèine. Its Cairene version was that of a provincial city beset by dust and flies, feeling faded, the windows in need of cleaning. In need of cleaning: this could be the epitaph of the Egyptian Museum too, where I watched a peon (as they are called in India) with the same stick with large squeegee used to clean floors—this one with a dirty rag wrapped around it—balance precariously on a ladder to swab at the dust of a year or two on the huge glass box containing the gold-plated shrine that in turn had contained the smaller shrine and this in turn the multiple mummy casings of the boy-King Tutankhamen, themselves displayed in the adjoining room whose temperature was ten degrees higher

than the cavernous halls of the rest of the museum from the crush of
sweating, insufficiently-clad tourists. The light fell through the skylights
and onto the huge glass box of the modern age protecting the wood and
gold box of thousands of years ago, light that was so necessary to showing off the gold at its best. And yet this glass surface, like the horizontal
surfaces of hundreds of other glass boxes in this too-full museum set up
by foreigners, had been left to become almost opaque with grayness now
being swabbed off in uneven streaks as I watched. The peon wrapped his
rag around a broom head and streaked up one pane out of a dozen. Then
he moved on to the next, the same by now filthy rag removing enough of
the dust for me to see the point of what he did, but still not to make the
glass clean.

Some of the side rooms of the Egyptian Museum are full of cases
with mind-numbingly repetitive fragments or endless mummy statuettes
of tombs lined up in row after apparently identical row. And then my
step slowed to a halt before a jaw-droppingly beautiful masterpiece: say,
King Tut's inlaid throne momentarily bereft of yakking guides—the king
and his queen with a single sandal each, sharing a pair to denote togeth-
erness, their bodies chunks of reddish semi-precious jewels; or, in another room, another floor, the commemorative statue of a woman
married to a dwarf, their two (apparently normal) children standing in
front of where the man's legs would have been on a normal pairing; or a
tiny ivory statue of the builder of the largest of the pyramids.

The tourists these days are different than they were the last time I
was here, 27 years ago. More numerous, to begin with—I have no memory of the crush of people at the beginning of the day at the Egyptian
Museum, though I visited nearly every day back then, a refugee from
pointless studies at the University of Munich, and staying with a friend
here in Cairo who worked during the day at the French Lycée and who
seemed glad to have me for company. The tourists also come from different places than they used to: their t-shirts say "Ukraine," or they talk
loudly in Russian. Yet the British, French, and Americans are reassur-
ingly the same, and all wearing fewer clothes than the people on the
street. What a sight to see a couple of Europeans walking along the Nile
clad not in the city clothes one would expect, but in shorts and sandals,
the women in tank tops. Where do they think they are? Clearly, in Africa.
For them this is vacation, and they are dressed accordingly. Different too
are the fact of the ubiquitous security checkpoints: one enters a metal
detector after every door (this is the country of bomb attacks against foreigners, though largely at the resorts in the Sinai)—though when it
beeps, that doesn't seem to alarm the guards, who wave one through;
where cameras are checked in every museum.

Since the last time I was in Cairo, there is also the fact that the local women have almost all put on scarves—the result of pressure from Muslim fundamentalists, we hear, or the general tenor of things. These haircovers have become simply the fashion, with gaggles of high school girls dressed in the regulation international skin-tight jeans and blouses, yet all swathed in the colorful head casings they must practice pinning so that they hug their faces. One woman in a hundred has the black shroud-like envelopment of the hijab, though here one sees the slit of eyes, rather than simply the overall covering of, say, Afghanistan; it's striking that the hands too are invisible, encased in black gloves. In the jaw-droppingly beautiful new Bibliotheca Alexandrina, a huge open area with the stacks moving down in giant-sized terraces under a floating ceiling to the Mediterranean and outfitted with all the latest technology, I watched a black-shrouded woman, her hands turned to glistening black by the gloves, pulling on her veil covering all but the slit of her eyes, which was impeding the mobility of her black-clad fingers on the computer keyboard. The bands of bearded young men who propound the veil say it's to protect the woman, and to allow her anonymity—as well as to eliminate the siren song of sex from the street, women being irresistible and leading men's thoughts astray. But in fact it screams "look at me." It renders not anonymous, but striking. Perhaps five women in a hundred still have the coppered hair and big hoop earrings of a Westernized Egyptian woman. For how much longer will this be possible?

The new Egyptian Puritanism has affected entertainment too, with belly dancers only in the international hotels, or in the restaurant boats bedecked with lights at night and silent in the morning as I run by, with only a few cabbage leaves on the sidewalk by the dozing watchmen to show the consummation that has taken place within—and few of them these days, I read, Muslim women. Instead, they are Russians, Bulgarians, and Albanians. On my last visit to Cairo I went with a gaggle of foreigners to L'Auberge des Pyramids—the photographs of that evening still lie somewhere in a pile of others in a drawer in Paris. The belly-dancer was Egyptian, the rolls of fat on her hips apparently part of the allure. At least the Saudi men at the other tables seemed to think so.

In need of cleaning: so too the zoo, many of the rusting old-style cages simply empty, the animals flea-bitten in others, the walkways garbage-strewn with families sitting in clusters on the intermittent grass. The cages in the zoo are like the empty and dusty glass boxes that seem so forlorn, here and there, in the Egyptian Museum, or the equally careless placing of statues in front of other statues. With so many things, and tourists whisked through to see the mask of King Tut and then hustled on their way, why bother to keep everything clean, everything in order?

Why a zoo? It seems like something someone long ago thought would be
a good idea.

Exiles

The particular cigarettes advertised on my pictures have long ago
ceased to be made, their Greek or Lebanese manufacturers only a memory evoked by pictures sold as artsy kitsch in a shop called *Nostalgie.*
But other cigarettes abound. In Alexandria we pass a visually decrepit
cigarette factory whose side proclaims "Eastern" in broken six-foot-high
letters. Its products, Ahmed tells me, assume many local names; the
building itself looks like a place the ill-fated gypsy Carmen could have
worked, its windows gaping—can it be that it is still functional? Ahmed
assures me it is. They need these factories, in whatever state of disrepair,
to keep up with the vociferous demand for cigarettes. People here smoke
everywhere, including in the middle of dinner, holding a cigarette in
front of them as they gesticulate. Men, and an occasional "liberated"
woman, puff away on the nargilas in cafes and coffee shops—I read in
the newspaper that a campaign is afoot to educate people to the fact that
a single pipe is the equivalent of smoking 100 (one hundred!) to 200 (!!)
cigarettes.

One of the people at a dinner in Alexandria holds a cigarette in my
face as I lean over the table, trying to understand what another is saying.
I make a face and wave away the smoke; he seems for the first time to be
aware that this might be distasteful and pulls his hand off the table. He is
Syrian and Italian, or perhaps Albanian... the man to whom I am talking
is Egyptian and something else. Turkish? The little old man with the
piercing blue eyes and the so-correct vest and hat across the table, M.
Albert, who says little, is (I am a bit confused regarding these people)
Lebanese. We speak Italian and French, and because these people are
proud of their English, English, in my honor. The Egyptian/Turkish man
(no, he must be Spanish, he's just come back from Madrid) is explaining
to me why suicide bombers do what they do.

We are told, he explains to me in jerking but continuous English, that
they blow themselves up from fanaticism. In fact it isn't that at all. Oh, I
say, to show politeness. What is it? I have to lean into the smoke to hear;
I would rather we spoke in a language he speaks without these odd cir-
cumlocutions, the strange intonation—I have to concentrate to block out
the cacophony around me, and to focus on the not-quite-center-of-the-
target English. Or is his Spanish better? Perhaps he isn't Spanish at all.

The man with the cigarette—by now he has finished the one that was
in my face, and has started another, though he holds it away—is (have I
got this right?) Syrian but married to an Italian. He can, that is, leave

Egypt. Ahmed, though born of a half-Italian mother, has an Egyptian father, and has no other possibilities, though he insists to me that he is Italian. Ahmed has spent much of his life attempting to gain Italian citizenship for himself and his now-elderly mother, who was born in Naples—for Ahmed the pinnacle of civilization—to a Turkish father and an Italian mother. All these half-and-half people are Ahmed's friends, or at least the acquaintances he wants to show off to me; in a sense, I am realizing, this get-together is in my honor. So my sense of confusion (who is half what and where do they live?) is mixed with embarrassment: at least I ought to get the people straight. I finally realize the woman sitting to my right is the Milanese wife of the Syrian smoker; I had taken her for Lebanese because she has been speaking in French. We switch to Italian, and I begin to get the relationships clear.

Yes, this is quite a gathering; I'm only now appreciating the effort Ahmed has gone to for me. He's called all his acquaintances here in Alexandria—"so much more beautiful than Cairo," he assures me, "just like Europe!" Earlier in the evening, in the charming and—here at least Ahmed is right—so-clean-it-could-in-fact-be Europe café where the group had met before dinner (it belongs to another Lebanese, who seems French to me), we had had hot chocolate, the best I'd ever drunk. Or am I simply seduced by the familiarity of it all, giving in to that greatest-of-all-expatriate compliments, "it's just like at home"?

Even now I have realized that all these people, or at least one spouse when there are pairs, are some of the flotsam abandoned behind the lines in Egypt at the breakup of the Ottoman Empire, or at least their descendents. Our host, as Ahmed assures me, is an "Italiano dell'Italia." That is, our host, though born in Egypt, has an Italian passport, and left Egypt as a young man, before the Revolution. Now, his hair white, he has returned to this side of the Mediterranean—after a career in what? Politics perhaps. He is comfortable here. He can leave, but has chosen to come back: his Alexandria is a city of memory in which he has come to live again.

The others have varying degrees of mobility. The Syrian, who by this point is already smoking, though more discreetly than he later does, is telling me of being condemned to three years in prison for refusing military service against Israel. He *thanked* the military judge, a colonel, something he reports to me with a pixie-like half-smile: it shocked the judge, who got upset and asked for an explanation. The next day, he tells me with no little self-satisfaction, he broke into the tribunal and destroyed his dossier. This story morphs into another about holding the records of an Italian company for three years (I'm not sure I get the point of this), of living off presents of thousands of dollars from Saudi princes, and of what, while working in Africa, he said to the president of Tanzania—complimenting "Mr. Nyerere for not giving his people the television." Mr. Nyerere responded, the careful, oddly accented voice telling the story, assures me, by saying: "My people are a simple people. They do not need the television."

How much of this am I dreaming and how much is real, how much true and how much invented or embellished for my benefit, here in this city of Alexandria from which the foreigners have been sent away, this meeting of half-Europeans with their stories of the days gone by? The "Italiano dell'Italia," with a mane of white hair and bad teeth, talks to me as we walk up deserted side streets—past the apartment building with the museum of Cafavy. He too seems to want to explain to me how it was, back in the old days, prior to the Revolution. When he was a child, everyone got along—this at any rate seems to be the gist of what I am agreeing to. (This part is in Italian, so there is not the strangeness of intonation of my Syrian/Egyptian, the one with the Milanese wife.) He is telling me that the Copts and Armenians simplified their food at home during the Muslim Ramadan, out of respect; how during the war, when the British interned the Italians, they Italian school children were let out with their Roman Catholic priest to attend the funeral of a Muslim holy man, all the groups clustering around the grave, the crosses, the priests, the imams, Orthodox, Jewish, Roman Catholic, and Muslim.

Caso di Riposo

This is the world of my cigarette advertisements for Greek and foreign manufacturers, a world preserved only in the memories of these people stranded here in Egypt, or having come back voluntarily, through the vagaries of princes and world politics. The next day I accompany Ahmed to the Caso de Riposo, a crumbling Italian palazzo with whose residents—twenty old men, largely half-stateless "Italiani dell'Egitto" without Italian passports, who can't leave—he has spent the night, depositing me at the Metropole by the Mediterranean to seek less costly quarters. We had met for breakfast, and had to go back to get his things. The aged gatekeepker and his decrepit dog let us in; the gardens are overgrown.

Inside, I am plunged into 1933. I know it is 1933 because a tombstone-sized marble tablet set in the wall informs me that Il Duce, Benedetto Mussolini, gave this building in "l'anno X de l'era fascista." Next to it hangs a sepia photograph of Il Re, Vittorio Emmanuele. Old men in pajamas, their white hair standing out uncombed from their heads, wander the cavernous halls.

The caretaker is a white-haired but still spry woman, an "Italiana dell'Egitto," with her equally white-haired husband. She chats affably and volubly: she spent 28 years with the five-year-olds up the street at the Collège de Saint-Marc, a neo-Gothic pile left over from the French with—I discover a half an hour later—its own marble commemorative tablets dedicated French priests who spent their whole lives here. The Collège de Saint-Marc has its own share of cavernous hallways, though these, in contrast to those at the Casa di Riposo, are full of light and people too young for riposo. I make a joke about going from the very young to the very old and the similarities between the two; the caretaker smiles in acknowledgment. She herself is not far off the age of those she takes care of. I ask how long the building we are in will remain as it is. She acknowledges that the residents simply die off, no new ones coming in—the "Italinai dell'Egitto" are a dying breed, and she is one of them. They have the lease until the year 2029, she says. (Which year of the fascist era would this be? I wonder idly, and am unwilling to do the math.) And then, "qui sa?" She spreads her hands. I doubt they'll even need it that long, I think.

Parenti

There is a law in Egypt, I read in the newspaper (there are at least two in English and one in French) saying that only Egyptians can lead around foreigners. This has produced problems for guides in non-standard languages few Egyptians speak; authorities are worried about getting Egyptian guides in languages like Finnish and Hungarian. The reason for the law is that non-Egyptians might say things that aren't flattering to Egypt. Beguilingly enough, this reason is printed for all to see and laugh, in the newspaper, as it would not have been in a half-way decent dictatorship, like the East Germany I knew from my time in Berlin. This is a country—Turkey is another—where insulting Egypt (in Turkey: Turkishness) is a crime. But I don't get the impression that many of the tourists read these newspapers, even though they're in the accessible languages of English and French. They have to catch their bus or their flight, or want to read the *International Herald Tribune*.

Ahmed gets into trouble repeatedly for another reason too: apparently it's also illegal for an Egyptian to walk with a single non-Egyptian—I'm not quite sure how the law is worded: groups are mandatory, individuals are prohibited. There has been much heated discussion at the entrance to the Cairo Citadel, a construction of the ruler known in the West as Saladin. Ahmed summarizes for me as we walk away: he has assured them that "siamo parenti," we're related, and is much put out.

I come to believe that Ahmed at least partly believes I am in fact his Italian cousin. He, after all, is, at least in his own mind, Italian—not like "these Egyptians," questi Egiziani. Later, taking off our shoes before the mosque of Al-Azar, he tells me his first degree was from the Muslim university of Al-Azar. The Copts in high places saw this, and refused him a job. Those Copts. So he got a second degree, this one from the (secular) University of Cairo. He simply leaves the Al-Azar degree off his CV, he tells me. I try to enter into the spirit of things and ask if the Islamic degree didn't give him an advantage with Muslims.

"Per niente," he says. "The one is worse than the other, Copts and Muslims." He himself is Muslim, lecturing me on having a beer, but not interrupting our perambulations to pray, asking me several times if I really, truly, deeply believe in God. I say I do. He says he does too. God has brought his miserable father (who was unkind to the mother and left the family) to a deservedly painful end, but was merciful to his well-liked brother, who died rapidly and fairly painlessly of bilharzia, a snail-borne river parasite that destroys the liver.

As Italians, we are forbidden from doing many things permitted to others, as Ahmed is continually having to point out to me. On Sunday we entered the walled old city—all the shops closed along the uneven dirt track of the main drag, in any case too close to the medieval northern gate for tourists—and found huge bags of garlic, human-sized and bulging with cloves bunched together sticking out all sides of their mesh, the air thick with the pungent smell of the snow-white bulbs. Ahmed tells me these are the wholesalers; they sell to the merchant people we are to see the next day, further on in the choked, chock-a-block-with-women-buying streets (chock-a-block on every day, that is, but Sunday, this one). But even in the right place on the right day, Ahmed won't let me buy the produce I thought we'd come to get—though the strawberries, for starters, looked delicious. He explains that nothing here along these market streets is good. First class things are exported, he informs me; second class go to the tourist hotels; third class are sold on the street. Apparently we'd just come to see. But he knows where to get better things. In fact, I never get my strawberries.

Later I want to buy a fruit juice in what looks to me like a proper shop on the street full of oranges and mangoes. Ahmed jumps a foot in the air when I suggest it. "Mai," he insists. Never! And then an explanation of how they don't wash the glasses well (I know this is true, I see them swish them in a bucket—but that's the way they do it in bars in the West, I silently object), Mama says never to etc.; we can get better things elsewhere. I protest silently, but know the fight wouldn't be worth it. Somehow I survived two years of Rwanda armed with nothing but common sense, after all. Later, he triumphantly hands me a bottle of local Orangina he's pulled from a shop's fridge: this, I realize, is the fruit juice (in fact all sugar water) that's better than the squeezed oranges I wanted, something worthy of Italians. I say I'm no longer thirsty.

Respect

I come to realize that a heated conversation of up to a quarter of an hour at every museum or monument is *de rigeur* for Ahmed, rather than simply paying and entering. Ahmed thinks he should be let in free, being an archeologist. As he explains to me with no apology, his claim to that title is that he did a "licensia" (B.A.) at the University of Cairo. When we walk down the main drag of the walled Islamic city, he tells me he passed his exam on this street, and tells me about the buildings. Some he's forgotten the names of.

In the world I come from, having a B.A. in Islamic architecture doesn't mean you should get into, say, the Greco-Roman museum for free—or indeed, any museum. But apparently in this world, it does. At every museum Ahmed tells his story, explains (so he later tells me) how he is an archeologist here with his Italian cousin. Plus he knows the director. I didn't believe Ahmed knew the directors of all these various museums, any more than I've allowed myself to enter his fantasy that I am his Italian cousin. Is his world of "archeologists" so small he actually could know these people? Or does he "know" them in the sense in which I could, under certain circumstances, if facts were different than they are, actually be his Italian cousin? Whatever the situation, the claim seems irrelevant to me. Yet the fact that he is received civilly, listened to, let in free, and in many cases even provided with a guide—the ultimate mark of respect in this world, it seems, though hellish for me, who would much rather visit alone—suggests to me that others find such claims valid currency.

It's not about money. At least, not for him. He'd pay the Egyptian rate; I'd have paid the foreigner's. Had I not already gone through all the stages of outrage and shoulder-shrugging acceptance to this un-American notion of two entrance rates in India, which does the same thing—it's the more un-American in that it's not enforced by passport, but by skin color; New Yorkers of Egyptian extraction pay the local rate—I'd be more than amused at the carefully marked "foreigner's" price, twenty times that of the Egyptian. No; it's about the respect. Along the way he invariably gets my fee halved to the student fee: I can't not be a foreigner, it seems, but I can be made instantly younger, like Faust.

Outside the so-called Pompey's Pillar in Alexandria (actually a pillar of Diocletian, who massacred so many of the Christians, they themselves having pillaged the antique Library of Alexandria), Ahmed's quest for respect takes its usual form: archeologist, knows the director, enter without paying. Here too it works. On the way out, when one of the Tourist Police (special police whose job is to look after such as me) has a lengthy conversation with him while I idly watch the traffic pass. Ahmed hauls out a piece of paper and writes something down. Finally he comes over to me (he's in no hurry for any of these interactions; they're the point after all). I ask what that was about. Oh, says Ahmed, the policeman is from another area of the country and wants to be transferred there. He's invoked Ahmed's help. Ahmed, glad to play protector, has noted his name.

So this really is how this world works, I think—insisting on others dancing attendance, freebies given because of whom one knows, who one is, offering (and perhaps even delivering) protection in return. This is certainly the garden variety of the corruption everyone agrees gnaws at the heart of Egypt. How much influence-peddling and strong-armed tactics, I suddenly wonder, stand behind every one of these unfinished holes in the forest of soaring concrete up by the Montaza Palace, where the Mediterranean crashes so dramatically in arcs of spray? Yet then I wonder: how else to navigate in a world where so many want what so few can get?

Military Museum

I said "Good morning" and "hello" to all the drowsy guards toting AK-47s at the entrances to the Nile restaurant boats as I ran by in the gray Cairo morning; they seemed eager to say "hello" back. In fact, such gun-toting guards are everywhere—in front of every shop, every bank, and apparently randomly spaced down every street. The result is that all of Egypt seems militarized.

Or perhaps I have become convinced this is so only because Ahmed's insisting on dragging me through the entire Military Museum in the Cairo Citadel that defines the city's skyline with the nineteenth-century mosque of Pasha Mohammed Ali. (In the Citadel, Ahmed's spiel has produced fifteen minutes with the director, who sat in the shade of giant umbrellas and talked on his cell phone while I wandered about, bored and restless; here I think he only knew someone who knew the director, but it was enough to get us both in for free and produce this reception, time-consuming for the higher-ups if pro-forma.) I'd tried saying I wasn't interested, but Ahmed pressed and I gave in—reasoning, here as elsewhere, that I'd probably learn something from the experience, even if it wasn't what I had in mind—learn, that is, something about Egypt if not about the thing I thought I was interested in.

And of course, as I always do with Ahmed (whenever else would I have gone to the Caso di Riposo in Alexandria? When to the ornate headquarters of the Egyptian Bank, the Bank Misr?) I do learn some-thing. The palace, given the fact that it was built in a former Ottoman province, turns out to be once again a local variant of the architectural mother lode of its period, Istanbul's Dolmabahçe Palace: all gilding, crystal, and hugely high painted plaster ceilings. And it's a surprisingly spiffy museum, as fresh and crisp as the Egyptian Museum is tired and abandoned-feeling. Military museums seem to rule in this city: this one is as well cared-for as the made-over Abdin Palace in the center of town, whose gardens are meticulously maintained, its former royal living quarters now filled with lovingly displayed and perfectly lit weapons: cases of swords and guns (Ahmed's favorite was Mussolini's pistol). Though there are virtually no visitors to tread on the red carpets or to stay behind the velvet ropes here in the Citadel's Military Museum, all are well-kept, sharp-edged, and spruce, with well-dressed guards wearing suits and the Easter-egg-colored ties that are clearly all the rage, and that I found so irresistible I bought half a dozen.

The Abdin Palace isn't so off-putting as the Citadel's Military Museum, however, its rooms of bejeweled guns seeming only like collecting gone mad. Here, the huge rooms with their velvet chairs house (indoors!) the ugly gray bores of cannons and ack-ack guns from World War I, blobs of ugly killer metal that are wildly out of place under the ornate ceilings and painted plaster. Painted dioramas of battles with exploding shells and mortar fire fill entire side-rooms off of what were clearly once reception chambers; endless busts of identical generals line endless hallways once meant for courtiers. Egypt has not won many battles in the last half-century, so the subjects of the dioramas have to be picked carefully. The cards in fractured English nonetheless extol the bravery of the Egyptian army, showing it storming beaches under fire and always emerging victorious. The victory over Israel of 1973 (according to most outsiders, not a victory but a "victory": an initial flush followed by defeat) figures heavily.

Ahmed calls me back from where I have been wandering too fast, my eyes blurring at the busts of generals—this is one of the endless hallways. I am annoyed that he's afraid I've missed something, but as it turns out, I have. He's showing me a model in wood of the Alexandria memorial to the Khedive Ishmael which we are to see the next day in Alexandria. The Khedive was a Europeanizing ruler of Egypt in the nineteenth century in the line of kings that ended only in 1953; the last king of Egypt was the infant son of the deposed King Farouk, named Fouad II, who "reigned" for less than a year. As the model shows, what properly belongs in front of the half-round colonnade as originally conceived is the statue of the Khedive. Under Nasser the statue was carted away (later it was erected by the Roman ruins across from the train station; the next day Ahmed points it out) and the colonnade—given by the Italians, Ahmed informs me—was used as the backdrop for the Tomb of the Unknown Soldier. Ahmed is highly disapproving.

Outside, in the courtyard, huge bas-relief sculptures set in the walls and towering over us as I sit and eat a protein bar while Ahmed politics in an office show Egyptians at various stages of their military development. The leftmost one shows the Pharaoh in a chariot, then comes the one with Islamic soldiers with scimitars, then the Ottomans, then the soldiers of World War I in their shaving-basin helmets, then the modern day. All history exists to end in the present. The sun, even by this time in mid-March, is relentless across their surfaces, picking out each exploding rocket, each falling enemy.

Garbage City

By this time I know that Ahmed's Egypt is seen through the prism of vanished foreigners and deposed royalty: everywhere he sees traces of King Farouk and King Fouad I (he prays in front of Fouad's tomb in the al-Rifai mosque down the hill from the Cairo Citadel); we visit palaces and talk about the decline of things under Nasser. Ahmed approves of Mubarak, he explains to me: Sadat and Mubarak at least brought peace with Israel, which has allowed some degree of economic upswing and better lives for all.

Ahmed isn't the only person I talk to who thinks the good old days were better; of course I'm meeting his acquaintances or friends, or his family members, who tend to see things his way. On our way from the Italian Embassy, where he has been unsuccessful in finding an Italian he's friends—or at least acquainted—with ("un Italiano dell'Italia"), and where we've been turned away by an intercom, left outside the gate, we pass into Garden City, a formerly lush area of town now gone to seed, as so much else in Cairo. In front of one building he observes that his great-aunt lives here; should we say hello? It seems so last-minute I wonder for a moment if he's kidding; he isn't. We wait in the cold hallway behind a metal grille. He rings, an old lady's face appears behind the grille: "It's Ahmed," he says loudly. There is no response but the closing of the door behind the grille. "She's unlocking," Ahmed informs me. This turns out to be true.

We are ushered into a cavernous flat with hugely high ceilings, furnished with the simpering niads of the antiques shops. Ahmed's aunt, he tells me, is Turkish—clearly in this world a thing devoutly to be wished. She seems pleased to see him, and shuffles away in house slippers to get us each a lukewarm Pepsi while I admire the ambience: nothing changed since 1950, at the height of royal/Egyptian-Ottoman-French splendor. All faded, of course, with the too-loud floral chair covers coming off. I re-arrange one, and the old lady—who speaks more than passable English, a relic of her dead husband's time as an administrator under the British—thinks I'm interested in what's underneath. She shows me: needlepoint chair covers. I express admiration; this is clearly the right thing to do, as this produces a tour of the apartment through the needlework framed and on the walls, or on chairs, that she herself has done. I feign astonishment mixed with courtly deference—all this *you?*

Yes, she nods, pleased. All this her. "Oh, so long ago," she says. "Back when this was a nice place to live."

I make a neutral moue.

"Yes," she insists, "Cairo *was* a lovely city." The emphasis is on the verb tense.

I know she is invoking the city that Ahmed is continually trying to cause to emerge, with his explanations, from behind the shabbiness, the dirt, the loud advertising signs, and the ugly new concrete buildings put up adjacent to more gracious ones. This building, he is always telling me, was a palace of the Pasha this, there the palace of the Princess that; here a street that has been re-constructed, there a statue removed and this and that altered. And he succeeds: I see the layers of his memory.

"Garden City," she says contemptuously. "This *was* Garden City. Now do you know what we call it?"

I shake my head on cue, amused at playing a part in this visit to the past.

"Garbage City," she says. "You wouldn't believe the people on the streets."

After a time she and Ahmed get to talking, in Arabic. I try to act interested in my surroundings without being nosy. I see a black-and-white picture of a bride, and assume it's her. I figure I can legitimately show interest. The picture is dusty, a somewhat thin-faced feline young woman, all in sepia. "What a lovely bride!" I say when Ahmed's conversation flags, feigning more admiration than I feel. (I can follow its gist from the proper names: Alexandria, Bruce, Hotel Metropole, Caso de Riposo, and so on.)

The old lady takes this as a provocation. "Not me!" she insists. "My daughter!" Her tone is sharp, almost reproving. However she offers me a reprieve. "Do you want to see a really beautiful bride?" Of course I say "yes" and she scuffles away, re-appearing a minute later with a badly-framed picture from which she is wiping the dust. "Now *this*," she says triumphantly, "is a beautiful bride."

I set my face in an appreciative smile and take the picture, then feel my heart drop a foot. She's not kidding. This bride, herself, is astonishingly beautiful—the daughter, as the mother well knows, isn't even in the same league. She's not simpering at the camera, but standing there with her equally attractive husband, decked out in his tarboosh (not outlawed here in Egypt, unlike in Turkey, simply laid aside at some point subsequent to this photograph as unmodern). And she's gorgeous. Jaw-droppingly gorgeous. I try to give her the reaction she deserves and knows she has a right to without being overly effusive. "Yes," I say. "This *is* a beautiful bride." And then I kid her about how she should give a party to show off the chair covers, and put this picture in the front hallway where her guests have to take off their coats, and when they ask who it was, say airily, oh yes, that's me of course. Now, however, her gray fly-away hair needs do-ing; she shuffles around in her carpet slippers; she spends the whole day in her cavernous apartment while the world grows less appealing outside.

When we leave I kiss her hand; I figure she's about as old-school as I'll ever meet, and will understand. It seems to have been the right thing to do; Ahmed kisses her hand as well, and she shows us to the door, apparently pleased. In the hallway there is some back and forth where she wants us to take the lift downstairs. I never take lifts even up if I know what floor I'm going to (I've walked up while Ahmed rode) and certainly not down: she's flummoxed, and Ahmed has to explain (he thinks it's strange too, as beneath my dignity), I don't follow as it's in Arabic, but the explanation must have been satisfactory as she smiles and waves and then disappears behind her grille and closes the door. What would her day have been like without our visit? I wonder.

Corniche/Sphinx

In Alexandria Ahmed has had a good idea: ride the mini-van taxis along the cornice. In the mini-vans there is quite a developed etiquette, I realize when I get in an almost full one and try to sit further forward than the backmost empty seat: I am waved back with rapid disapproving explanations. Then I find I've entered a sort of slow-motion forward-wave of arms: the money ballet. People hand their folded over and apparently much-used single pound (20 cent) notes up to the front by draping their arms, their hands clutching the money, over the shoulders of the people in front of them. The people in front, unsurprised at seeing arms clutching paper suddenly hovering by the side of their faces, reach out and absent-mindedly move the money forward by doing the same to the person in front of them.

I'm sitting by the window, so the goings-on inside the van don't impede my view of the Mediterranean. Still, it helps that I know what's there already. I'd gone running at daybreak along the slick wave-spattered stones of the Corniche, watching the seedy buildings give way to the Tomb of the Unknown Soldier (stripped of its proper statue, I knew) and then to the over-florid modern mosque, and then the stinking-of-fish fishermen's strip, past the excavations where the few tourists there are are invited to visit the underwater excavations of "Cleopatra's Palace"—the source of eerie photographs I later saw in the Alexandria National Museum, divers swimming around statues still proffering their pots to the fishes, their heads cocked as if seeing something on the ocean floor.

Apparently these waves of money-passing, these mosh pits of paper, was the way all public transportation works, not just the mini-vans. Back in Cairo, or more precisely the sister city of Giza (rather like Cambridge to Cairo's Boston), Ahmed and I take a trip out to the Pyramids on a proper bus where I stand, but am too tall to have much of a view outside, my head protruding into the covered part of the bus. All I can see is the continuous wave of money changing hands just below my eye-level while the people propelling them go on with their conversations. And then suddenly we get out, in a village. Before us, abruptly, are the Pyramids. It's not how I remember from 27 years ago: then perhaps the village wasn't so close, or I was able to see more getting there—it's a normal road, with normal shops. And then the desert starts.

A tourist policeman sits on a camel silhouetted against the Pyramid of Cheops. Two American girls clown for photographs inside the nearby tomb of a lesser mortal. The Sphinx (as the Greeks called it; there's apparently no evidence it was such to the Egyptians) is covered with birds that make its head look as if dotted with the remains of plugs of hair, like the head of too dearly loved dolly back home my wife has saved from her childhood, and that I finally put a hospital newborn knit hat on to hide the broken off tufts.

Down the hill and past the Sphinx, the road turns touristy: there are many groups of school girls, all with colorful scarves over their hair, and pre-adolescent boys. All say "Hello where are you from?" or "Hello what's your name?." I smile and wave. I wish I'd remembered my hat. I'm sweating, and it's only mid-March. The dust has already begun to turn the green leaves of the trees beside the road the gray color of lizard's eyes. It is the brief Egyptian spring; soon summer will start.

Intimations of India

1.

India: the very name still means exotic in the West. Pearls, elephants, and Raj—as well as disease, famine, and the poor. Virtually no one from the West can come to India without being prepared for Something Different. Yet at the same time it's real for me, not vacation. I've come to give lectures at universities—institutions Western in origin, long-since become Indian. Am I an outsider to this country or am I simply doing my job in a new place? I am to speak in English, a European language that is certainly not a foreign language here, even if spoken by a tiny minority of the population. (The one aspect of Indian civilization that nearly every author I have read mentions is its syncretic nature, the way India subdues invaders by assimilating them, englobing them like an amoeba.) How to separate the familiar from the different? Everything here is fair game for the aesthetic sense of life, as it is not at home—though much of it will be discarded as being simply the same. I have to keep my eyes and ears open, ask questions, and stab at generalizations as best I can. Though it's a sort of blindman's buff, the process has its own exhilaration. The alignments here will come from too much new information, not—as it frequently seems at home—too little.

India has changed in the first decade of the new millennium: suddenly India is an economic up-and-comer. India and China, we hear, though India seems less relentless than China—being, after all, a democracy. These Information Technology palaces we read about—how do they fit into the rest of the landscape? What of the fact that when I call in Washington about my credit card bill, I like as not get a young man on the other end who's up in the middle of his night at a "call center" in Bangalore, his carefully imitated American accept startling in its breeziness and only through occasional lapses betraying that it is in fact Bangalore he's talking from (I always ask) and not Boston? How much has this fact changed the world around it? These connections with the outside are themselves part of the tapestry.

I arrive at the Bombay airport in the wee hours of the morning, my sleep torn by time change, the endless drab airport overexposed in fluorescent light. On the way down to the end of the Colaba peninsula, the center of the old part of town, we careen around empty and yellow-lit corners on which, though it is now the middle of the night, wilt a few forlorn soldiers. Because of terrorists and the troubles in Kashmir, says the driver. We pass what seem to be whole sleeping cities of squatters' dwellings, makeshift tents made of piles of rags. Later, in the daylight hours, I see tangle-haired women squatting over fires, nursing children, and carrying on with their lives. This is different.

My airplane ticket says Bombay, but the city has re-baptised itself Mumbai, in the local language, Marathi. Some people, I am to understand, think this is a blow for independence, rejecting the British influence of this built-by-the-British city. To me it seems odd that a local language can trump the international designation, as if Detroit were to get itself officially renamed Motown. It's part of the current wave of Indian mania to rename—Calcutta has been re-phoneticized Kolkata, and Madras is now (once again, it's claimed) Chennai—each in the language local to its area. (Later I'm told all aer like the Chinese insistence that Peking be re-phoneticized as Beijing. Yet the French have refused to adopt this, and in any case it's not a regional language issue, but one of how the Mandarin is written.)

Finally we are on a main street. Beyond, we see a curving line of lights along the water: Queen's Necklace, the driver tells me, Marine Drive. This cornice road, I know, has another Indian name as well, given after Independence in the last wave of name changes. Yet I am to find, the attachment to the old British names is strong for the streets too as well as the cities, and the streets have been changed longer ago than the city names. In the course of my visit I go to the Prince of Wales Museum in Bombay, which has another name too that nobody remembers—a triumph of Indo-Saracenic architecture, all onion domes and Moorish arches; in Trivandrum (Indian version: Tirivuananthapuram), the University where I am to speak is across from the Victoria Jubilee Hall; in Madras, the main thoroughfare is still referred to by its old name, Mount Road, despite having a more modern Indian one which no one uses.

Then I am being handed out of the car at the Taj Mahal Hotel—a grand Victorian monument that all visitors seem to remember fondly—by a Sikh doorman in a turban and greeted by beautiful women in saris clicking across the marble floors in high-heeled sandals. This name has not changed: it is "the Taj" to all who know it; no one here, I learn, thinks of the Moghul mausoleum it's named after.

The next morning, dragging myself from bed into the semi-darkness of the beige-walled room, I open my curtains to a breathtaking view of the harbor and the Arabian Sea, invisible in darkness the night before but now dotted with ferries. When I leave my room (the stationary having assured me that this is "The Most Prestigious Address in India"), the contrast between the air conditioning and the steam-bath in the three-stories open courtyard outside is so strong that my glasses immediately fog up. After breakfast (I could be anywhere in the world in this buffet room; indeed I wonder for a minute if I am not back at the American hotel in Frankfurt where I had spent the previous night) I head towards the Gateway of India, a huge sandstone arch commemorating a 1911 visit by

King George, who came to be crowned Emperor of India. I am looking
for the departure point of the boats to Elephanta Island, one of my "must-
see" tourist destinations during this initial week-end. I have been told
that during the monsoons—such as now—the boat service is interrupted,
and I am eager to take advantage of a clear day. I need not really look,
since I am immediately accosted, as I hurry across the square, by one of
the ferry's captains who, spotting a tourist, takes me in hand and sells me
a ticket for a boat he is anxious to get underway.

Among the earliest monuments of Hindu civilization to come to
Western consciousness, I have read in John Keay's fascinating *India
Discovered*, are the temples on the island in Bombay's harbor that the
British baptized Elephanta, after the huge stone elephant found there now
in the Victoria Garden. (This is not too far from the huge towers where
the Paris, Indians of Persian descent and worshippers of the fire god
Zoraster, expose the bodies of their dead to be picked clean by vultures:
The Towers of Silence, they are called in eerie poetry.) The local name
of the island, however, is quite different; Garapuri.

The boat, though chugging along at a good speed, takes an hour to
reach its destination. I pass the time looking at the nearby island covered
with oil refiners, at the Bombay skyline receding in the haze behind us,
and at the people. A boy and girl near the bow hold hands and whisper. I
am to see relatively little of such different-sex pairs in the next weeks, far
more common being two men linked by a pinky or an arm as in Arab
countries or the south of Italy. The group of young men in sandals who
comprise most of the small number of passengers becomes excited when
a helicopter bearing the insignia of the police hovers overhead, spraying
us with droplets from the water its blades are stirring up. Finally, its play
over, it flies off to another ferry that is steaming back to the city and dogs
this one for a while. Good sport, everyone seems to feel; clearly they are
disappointed when it leaves.

I disembark from the large boat onto a smaller one which takes us to
the slippery pier. Realizing the inevitability of choosing a guide—this is
not tourist season; the guides are many and the tourists few—I allow a
barefoot man wearing a shirt and dhoti, whose English I can mostly understand, to take me on. After agreeing on a price, he immediately proves
his worth by fending off other comers.

My guide talks as we walk up the steep path on this verdant island:
normally he works in the rice paddies, but the rains are slow this year.
This is supposed to be monsoon season but no one knows where the
monsoon has gone. The reservoirs are dangerously low; people have begun to fear for their crops. Later, my university friends assure me that
there is no danger of factual famine—in recent years the government has

erected silos of emergency grain rations and dotted them throughout the country. On the other hand, they say, malnutrition is endemic; hygiene standards in the villages are lamentable. Even in the large hotels one does not drink the water that comes from the tap: In every room there are flasks or plastic bottles of drinking water on the table. My guide has grown up on Elephant and later points down to a fishing village on the coastline: home, he says.

The Great Cave—not a cave but a temple carved out of living rock, consisting of hallways with multiple pillars from around which the stone has simply been removed, is eerie with filtered light and reflections from the tank that is part of the temple, serving as a reservoir of rainwater for the local people. This temple is considerably more complex than others on the island, and contains—I have read—some of the finest sculpture in India, as for example the huge bas-relief of Shiva in his three faces of creator, destroyer, and preserver: the imposing Shiva Mahesamurti that towers out of the semi-darkness over the mortals before it. Many of the guardian figures on the prison-cell-like lingam shrine in the center of the hallway are missing parts and even entire bottom halves; the Portuguese, I had heard, used this hall for target practice.

My guide bows before the lingam in the shrine, the smooth rounded post that is the phallic symbol of Shiva, glistening black with oil and topped with a handful of rather touching wildflowers. To one side I hear the chattering of monkeys who, when I leave the temple, scamper across my path, the babies clinging to the fur on the mothers' underbellies. The guide shows me the level the water in the tank should normally have reached; a chute of corrugated aluminum guides what rain there is towards the collection tank. As I leave the island for the boat I buy postcards in faded colors in spongy cardboard; clearly my guide is disappointed that I have not bought more from the row of trinket and refreshment sellers that make a gauntlet of the path down to the pier.

The next day at this time I am at the Crawford Market, Bombay's central market, looking for something a friend has asked for that, I discover, dos not exist in India; curry powder. Instead, I buy plastic bags of constituent spices that the vendors assure me must be mixed for curries, along with a tiny box with a garish picture of the goddess Lakshmi containing exactly one gram of dark yellow shreds of saffron. I am too late in the day to seem much of that portion of this great over-structure devoted to the slaughter and carving of meat; it is already afternoon and all that is left when I stick my head in the shadowy concrete hall are bloody slabs and crows swarming over piles of bones. The butchers, who have been up since the middle of the night, are taking a nap on the ground. Later in traffic my taxi nearly runs down a man trundling a wheelbarrow full of bloody haunches and thighs that he undoubtedly bought here, one of the army of middlemen who transform wholesale to retail. He looks neither right nor left, merely pushing his barrow in front of the oncoming cars and motorbike-rickshaws and assuming, as most pedestrians clearly do in this country, that he will simply be avoided. It works for the cows, after all, that wander and lie at all, even in the middle of the busiest highways—why not for humans? I think of how his bloody wares are surely absorbing all the choking fumes of the diesel and kerosene-run rickshaws; he disappears from sight onto a pedestrian island that he shares, for a brief moment, with two sleeping cows and one sleeping man.

Indeed, the streets of Indian cities are an adventure in themselves, and I soon learn to cower in the back of my taxi and hope for the best. The landscape is especially animated in the older town centers, such as in the heart of Hyderabad's Charminar district, where Muslim women swathed in black swirl around roadside vendors of flowers, bananas and apples, and bangle bracelets. Pedestrians walk at their own speed, usually cross the flow, bullock carts poke along and change course at will, rickshaws dodge in and out, cars barrel at each other headlong in passing the slower-moving objects, swerving out of the way by micro-seconds. The result is like films of the cells in the bloodstream: hundreds of particles hurtling forwards at breakneck speeds down a narrow causeway. In my time in India, nonetheless, I am to see only a single accident, and this does not seem to have been fatal. I leave thinking that the same laws of physics cannot apply here, or that these so-sturdy Ambassadors and Premiers are not made of iron but of rubber, and bounce rather than crash. In fact, many people each year die in traffic accidents; I have merely been spared the sight of any.

The assault on the senses does not neglect the aural. Each of the muffler-less three-wheeler rickshaws that darts in front of my taxis in four cities bears the injunction "Please sound horn," or simply the less polite "Sound Horn" or the step-by-step version, "Horn OK Go." I am at first puzzled by what seems this positive invitation to brouhaha, and ask my taxi driver what it means. He explains to me that before passing, other drivers are to sound horns so that the rickshaw knows to move over. This is reasonable, I think, but I discover that the result is a continuous cacophony of motor horns, to the point where driers honk, it seems, to reassure themselves of their own existence: on almost empty highways (no highway is completely deserted: people walk, cows wander in the most empty of places) drivers keep up what seems a constant conversation with the trees and other cars, even acknowledging bumps in the road with a friendly honk or two.

The air in the meat section of Crawford Market is heavy, and I'm not sorry to withdraw from this darkened butchers' barrio smelling of blood and the stickiness of death. The vegetable and fruit sections of the great arched iron arcade are more aesthetic, full of the fragrances of piled mangoes and guavas, the mounds of apples from the Himalayas that I was surprised to see. I had even bought a bag of apples on my way through Germany, thinking they would make good travel food and reflecting I would surely not see apples for weeks. The apple season is brief, I'm told, even in the mountains—and was somewhat consoled. In the flower stalls men twist jasmine into garlands for statues of the gods, and for women's hair. Many times in the ensuing weeks I violate the norms of propriety by edging up to women to smell the snow-white flowers twisted in their black hair, though in fact I need not get so close: the smell of these heady flowers is so penetrating that their introduction into even a large room is immediately detectable. One night I place in a saucer of water a few jasmine flowers I have collected, and awake to a pile of wilted petals and a plate full of odorous liquid.

The walkways of the Crawford Market are chaos, but somehow appealingly so—probably because I am at least six inches higher than virtually anyone here. Men carrying packets of fruit on their heads bump and criss-cross, hurrying by on the straw and mud that covers the flooring. In the stalls beneath the counters where men lie stretched out sleeping re sub-tenants sitting cross-legged on the ground, at the level of my ankles but well out of harm's way: largely flower-stringers, usually women with their children, working away just inches away from a forest of legs and feet.

In exiting I fight off beggars, or rather, ignore them. This, I find, is the way Indians do it: how often will I hear friends say with no little justice, accompanying me along city streets, "You can't give to them all"? At intersections, armies, armies of ragged boys descend on cars—here, the playthings of the rich—to smear at their windshields with rags in hopes of a few small coins. "It just encourages them to leave school," my friends will say, somewhat apologetically, as they roll up the windows.

2.

No one goes to India for the first time without presuppositions: the aesthetic sense involves comparing the presuppositions with the perceived. In this, as in other things, India is like America, which for many Europeans is all cowboys, gangsters, sky-scrapers, and fast food—as well as large convertibles rolling along endless California highways. One of my images was being besieged wherever I went by positive armies of beggars. Yet in fact, things have not been so bad. To be sure, at tourist sites, people curved into strange shapes—the spider-shaped cripple at in front of the rock-carving called "The Penance of Arjuna" in Mahabalipuram on the Bay of Bengal a week later, for example, walking with two arms and two legs on the ground—come up hopefully, plying their own strangely mundane trade with each group of visitors, combining a freak show for which one pays with a request for alms. Women sit at the gateways of temples and mosques, holding out their hands at ankle-level, and the dark-skinned tribal children in the south approach foreigners outside of airports and train stations. India has numerous members of native tribes who escape the caste system completely, being even outside of the comfortingly certain designation of Untouchability; nowadays they are called Scheduled Tribes, as the former Untouchables are called Scheduled Castes.

Expecting the hoards of ragged little boys and girls who surround the white-skinned foreigner in central Africa, I am impressed by the fact that people here seem largely to go about their business, however rudimentary that may be, and leave others alone. Or is this simply evidence of the waxing hard-heartedness of increasingly capitalistic India, now well on its way to "liberalizing" its markets and opening to the West? In the early years, I read, there were many cases of huge investment fraud; I think of the American equivalent from the 80's and feel right at home, through friends shake their heads over the detrimental effect on investor confidence in a still youthful stock market.

Still, the poor are evident: there are the tangle-haired children of the squatters in Bombay's slums, the peasant wading knee-deep in mud through his tiny rice paddy behind the plow pulled by a bullock that I see in the surreal landscape outside of Hyderabad, near the University and strewn, at least the first time I saw it, with huge boulders. Nearby, in Hyderabad proper—and again in Kerala, on the Malabar Coast—I see what seem the lowest of the low: those people, largely women, who squat all day by the side of the road to reduce huge chunks of these same boulders to fist-sized rocks which another person beside them reduces to even smaller rocks; tapping and tapping away with tiny hammers, or with other rocks. At least they are not in the sun: each rock-tapping station has propped over it and leaning on a stick a huge palm leaf that provides shade. Ultimately these rock-tappers will all but clear the landscape around the University in Hyderabad, the rocks ground up for construction in the New India. Then, of course, there are the sweepers—men and women bent over the hand brooms made of palm spins whom I see neatening the dirt courtyards of houses as well as in city offices—and the latrine-emptiers, formerly a job only for Untouchables.

Occasionally, a Scheduled Caste or former Untouchable politician is elected to a ceremonial position in politics: India has what is surely the most extensive program of legally mandated "affirmative action" for its downtrodden of any country in the world, with carefully calibrated quotas for university slots and in government for members of what are sometimes called "backward castes." In America, I reflect, a country with similar problems, the very mention of quotas spells death for any politician accused of it. "Caste?" my Brahmin friends in response to my question as to whether caste is still widely talked bout: "people talk only of caste. Even when they don't talk of caste, they're talking of caste."

And indeed the question of caste clearly looms large. Determined to ameliorate the worst excesses of the caste system—a determination which began in Gandhi's program to remove the Untouchables, whom he called Harijan ("Children of God"), from their status as outcasts—newly independent India established these preferential quotas, originally scheduled only for ten years. Each ten years since independence, however, these have been renewed. Many Brahmins, I am to discover, routinely grumble that the education system is going to pot because the universities must admit so many Scheduled Caste students (my American ears have heard arguments like this before). Others, friends tell me, tend to feel guilty nowadays over the privilege they have enjoyed for millennia. Being a Brahmin, like being a straight white male in America, is no longer "in." An editorial in the newspaper *The Hindu* during my stay analyzes the caste system as a good idea originally based on merit and assuming individual mobility, that somehow ossified and became a system of birth. No one publicly defends this system any more in the Republic of India; nonetheless it seems to define a good many aspects of life here; the rise of the Hindu political party BJP seems to an outsider a response to this swing of the pendulum.

One of the aspects that caste still defines is marriage. I spend one whole Sunday morning reading the wedding advertisements in the *Times of India*. All are inserted by parents looking for a bride or a groom for their marriageable son or daughter. Most specify caste, sub-caste, ad community as well as linguistic group. (The lingua franca of the elite is English; Hindi fluency is limited to a band in the North that includes Delhi: in each city I stayed I was in the center of another regional language—respectively Marathi, Urdu, Telegu, and Malayalam, part of which goes to explain why English, despite public bad-mouthing by some liberal politicians, is in India to stay.) Such great number of the advertisements carry the assurance that the prospective bride is "convent-educated" that later I ask University friends if Christians in fact have the monopoly on education. No, they assure me, though there are convent schools; in a wedding advertisement this means only that the young woman in question is fluent in English.

Arranged marriages, I am told, are still the norm in the upper and lower classes in India, and still prevalent even in the middle class, where Western-style love-marriages have made the greatest inroads. India boasts a middle class nearly equal in size to the entire population of the United States, I read at one point, though it represents less than a fourth of the overall population of the country here. Yet middle class in India, I am to discover, means something different than in the United States or Western Europe as far as creature amenities go. Hand in hand with the arranged marriage goes the dowry. Until recently, the problem of "accidental" burning to death of brides whose dowries remained unpaid was a great cause for concern. Now the law has been changed to put the burden of proof on the husband in cases where the wife dies in the first years of marriage—a clear violation of constitutional rights, some of my friends pointed out to me, with a presupposition of guilt rather than of innocence.

Virtually all of these marriage advertisements, I was interested to see, specify skin tone in the spouse-to-be. Indeed, this is a society that is fully as conscious of skin color as the one I have left behind, and one where the obsession is far more honestly acknowledged. "Wheaten" is the most desirable complexion, which is to say light-skinned, though I am told it matters more for women than for men that they be light. For girls, "dark" is a term of opprobrium, though in a world of people in shades of brown, no one knows how the children will come out.

I'm perversely fascinated to find that the beauty ideal of this society is men and women who look like Southern Italians, or perhaps Lebanese. The garish, hand-painted and three-dimensional movie billboards in Bombay and Madras uniformly show people who would be at home on the streets of Rome. (India has the largest movie industry in the world and in all the local languages; though my intellectual friends repeatedly criticize the quality of these films, their sheer number and variety seemed to me impressive when compared to an American system that allows only the extremes of Hollywood blockbusters and low-budget independent films.) So too magazines like *Society* and *Cine-Blitz* that I buy along with *India Today* in the hotel bookshop (one of the cover stories in the former: "Shower Power: Don't be a Drip this Monsoon"), full of full-lipped "wheaten" beauties of both sexes.

It's some comfort to my overwrought liberal American racial sensibility to realize that this preference for light skin pre-dated the Europeans by millennia, being brought into a dark-skinned country by the fairer-skinned Aryan invaders from the north, who introduced Hinduism and the caste system to the native Dravidians. These were pushed southward, as well as being relegated to the lowest rungs of this system. India, I suggest to friends later as I ruminate on all of the various influences that have fed into it, seems like an onion: take away the layers of successive invasions—Aryan, Moslem, British—and nothing is left. They allow as I may be right. Still, Hindu nationalists seem bent on marginalizing the contribution of other groups to the Indian onion, specifically those of the Muslim "invaders." The next most obvious target is the British, though their institutions and buildings define modern India.

In addition to the divisions within Hinduism, there is the animosity that separates Hindu from Moslem: the newspapers are full of the ongoing negotiations regarding the Ayodhya mosque, built centuries ago by the Moghul emperor Babar on what Hindus have rather recently decided is the birthplace of Rama, hero of the semi-religious epic *Ramayana* and one of the avatars of Vishnu. Hindu agitation is demanding the destruction of the mosque and the erection of a temple; cooler heads, such as that of an editorial writer in *The Hindu*, are asking for a little education in comparative religion and a sharing of the site. Later, after the riots, I reflect that this education never came. Nor, I think, would a little education be amiss to bridge the increasingly gaping gaps in American society, the fundamentalist Christians against all the rest.

3.

India, I realize, is a fragmented society. The Partition that broke off Muslim Pakistan from secular but overwhelmingly Hindu India at Independence seems to be still felt as a wound by many Indians today: the break polarized things further, in that Muslims were forcibly displaced to Pakistan and Hindus to India. Still, more Muslims remain in India than in all of Pakistan. What, an outsider wonders, were those behind Partition thinking?

Pakistan is India's greatest military rival and foe. Hindu friends complain, with the acrimony that only sport can evoke, that Indian Muslims routinely cheer Pakistan in intra-subcontinental cricket matches; later, in Madras, my drier curves through a residential quarter of impressive villas behind walls dripping bougainvillea, and informs me that all these opulent houses belong to "Muslim smugglers." Indeed, even from an American perspective, it does not seem that Pakistan's military junta, that came to power in a coup and is one of America's most-rewarded allies, cares to do much about curbing its own form of terrorism—our American national priority since the destruction of the World Trade Center. Why, Indian friends ask me, do the Americans reward the Pakistanis

when they're so clearly harboring terrorists, and turn their back on a democracy, India? I have no good answer for this.

Christians are a tiny minority in India, though this religion, like so
many others, seems to have adapted well to India, and even flourished.
After all, as the Indians like to point out, parts of India were Christian-
ized long before Britain was. The statues of the origin in roadside shrines
are no less brilliantly painted than those of Shiva and Parvati or the ele-
phant-headed Ganesh who is so beloved in India (Headline in the *Times
of India*: "Ganesh Idols Flood Bombay," on an exhibition and sale of
thousands of statues of Shiva's popular son); the flowers draped around
the neck of the Virgin are the same as those offered to Lakshmi; indeed
Hinuism's equivalent of the infant Jesus is the Infant Krinsha—another
of the avatars of Vishnu (there are ten), usually shown with His mother.
Krishna is also worshipped in a form more alien to Western sensibilities,
namely not as a sexless child, but as a super-virile lover of a throng of
milkmaids, or gopis, who provide one of the recurring motifs of Hindu
art; Krishna himself is usually painted blue, and frequently plays a flute.

I was interested to see, in the originally Portuguese Cathedral of San
Tomé in Madras/Chennai—where according to doctrine the remains of
the Apostle Thomas, reputedly martyred on a hill outside the city now
near the airport, are interred under the altar—the same strings of lights
that decorate Hindu idols hanging before the statues. Here too the Christian faithful remove their shoes before entering, as do all visitors to temples and mosques. Here at San Tomé, the walkways outside are covered
with the same intricate designs in rice flour that I have seen outside
Hindu temples, and Christ is flanked on the altar by a pair of peacocks
indistinguishable from those sacred to Lakshmi, Vishnu's consort, that I
have seen in the great temple in Mylapore. India is indeed a syncretic
land.

Another church: St. Mary's Episcopal Church, in Fort St. George,
Madras. Madras was one of the first British settlements of the 17th century, and administration was from within the moated neo-classical pre-
cincts of the fort, now far to the north of the city. I tell the taxi driver
simply "Fort St. George," and passing the Gandhiji statue on the beach,
soon find myself in front of a gorgeous cluster of 18th century Georgian
buildings, a whole small city with a museum, a church, and a military
parade ground. Now it houses the state government of Tamil Nadu; only
the museum (room on deserted room of faded regimental flags, stray
pieces of French porcelain, and mediocre paintings of governors of Madras) and St. Mary's church can be visited. The latter turns out to be a
charming Christopher-Wren-like building, still the principal Anglican

church in Madras and, as a plaque at the gate tells the visitor, the oldest Anglican church east of Suez.

Its shaded churchyard is paved solid with tombstones of men and women whose life stories are told briefly or more fully in flowing, 18th-century script: businessmen here outside in the early years, mostly, and their wives and children, many of whom died young. So too the walls of the spare church inside: here changing fashions of death can be charted as 18th-century skulls give way to the broken columns and drooping willows of the Victorian era, and businessmen and their wives become rare among the 25-yearpold lieutenants who lost their lives to cholera and are mourned by the members of their company. I think of a similar church I have seen in Mombasa, on the Kenya coast, which is touching for the same reasons, and where similar plaques commemorate those who died, too young and far from home, in the cause of Empire, and of the plaques in Calcutta's Saint Paul's, many of whom fell victim to "The Mutiny" of 1857. (Some Indians call this the "first war of independence.") Here in St. Mary's, so the guidebooks note for the benefit of visiting Americans, was married one Elihu Yale, governor of Madras, later founder of the Connecticut university that bears his name. Scuffing away the leaves from a slab, I meditate as many have done before me on Death the great level of earthly differences.

Differences which are—I think many times each day during my time in India—extreme in this society. Clearly, in some ways, the Indian economy is hopping: real estate values for crumbling properties in Bombay/Mumbai are among the highest in the world. There are moderne buildings rising from what seem slums in the oddest places—outside of Bombay, the financial capital of India, but also in Hyderabad. I will be rattling along, careening around half-finished houses with itinerant workers camped in a settlement of tents with their children playing on the packed down dirt and their women clustered around the single faucet that serves all (there are no sanitation facilities; people simply go as far out as they can and squat, the women using darkness insofar as possible to cover their modesty) and suddenly there before me like a mirage will be an office building that would look at home in any mid-sized American city, surrounded by gates and parking lots.

Yet these islands of fluorescent coolness are as amenable to the inevitable power outages (several hours each day) as other buildings, unless they have their own generator, and can't produce anything that might have to travel over the impossible roads: hence the interest of IT for India. The cities lack any infrastructure past the day the British left, with their sanitation systems now serving many multiples of what they were planned for and the gutters overflowing at the slightest rain. One day I am shopping in Hyderabad. My driver comes rushing into the shop: Quick, he says, we have to go, the roads will flood and we'll never get home. As it is, we sit in bottlenecks and two-feet-deep water: every major city floods this way in the rains, sometimes with fatal consequences for the people. Mumbai flooded this way in 2005; many people died. And none of this development touches the half a billion illiterates, the peasants walking behind bullocks in the mud of their fields, or cooking over an open fire and balancing a baby on her hip—or those who have sought refuge in the cities, only to end up in squatter camps.

Situated above both the vast mass of the faceless poor and the aspiring middle class—a middle class that works in filthy warren-like offices, commutes hours to work on overcrowded trains, and lives in tiny city apartments with peeling walls an cockroaches where the cold water and electricity go off for hours at a time—is the tiny group of the very rich, those who got wealthy on industry in the post-independence years In India, the rich live very well indeed—better than in the West, I would say. For wealth here, in a country with a billion people and many people looking for jobs, means servants, and never having to lift a finger—not even to do the recreational chores America's wealthy, like gourmet cooking, or cutting the grass on a John Deere.

Though I try to tell myself that the rich are the almost infinitesimal minority in this country, the beginning of my visit at the Parsi- (Indian-) built Taj and my subsequent, if intermittent, stays in Indian-owned luxury hotels across South India make it difficult for me to convince myself of this fact. A friend remarks that well-to-do Bombayites treat the Taj, with its lounges, its pool, and its rows of luxury shops, like their private club. Indeed, the lobby and lounges are full of women in gold-embroidered saris (many priced, I discover, at a year's salary of a middle-class functionary), dropping ropes of pearls and with diamonds spraying from their ear lobes. One night a wedding reception is letting out as I ascend the stairs up the four sides of the huge square interior courtyard at the Taj's center: I pause by the room festooned with garlands of jasmine and roses to admire the beautiful people exiting from it covered in jewels and gold, the children of Tata (buses and heavy industry) and Bajaj (electronics and motor scooters) who make up contemporary India's version of rajas and ranis.

Not that the real maharajas and ranis have disappeared, though they have gone underground. Their titles officially abolished under Indira Gandhi, their states since independence merely part of the Indian Union, they nonetheless continue to designate the oldest son maharaja ("great ruler"), to marry their daughters off to the sons of other princes, and to lead their international, café-society-type lives. In Bombay I am invited to a dinner by American diplomats; they tell me the man in the other couple is the younger son of a maharaja; his wife is herself a princess. I wonder how to address them; my embarrassment is allayed at the introductions. As it happens, there's only the husband. Call me Shiv, he enjoins. I do so, and find myself talking with an urbane, graying man in athletic middle age, who combines moose hunting in Alaska with conservation efforts for a particular kind of lion native to his family's state.

Dinner is at the Willingdon Club on the outskirts of Bombay, all teak and whirring fans and armchairs. After the meal—a cosmopolitan mixture of veg and non-veg, Indian and Continental—we tour the rooms, overflowing with evidently well-to-do Indians lounging in wicker chairs. My hostess shows us the golf course, dark now at night but, she says, a verdant oasis of calm in a chaotic city during the day. We tour the ballroom, now deserted. She points out as well the naked light bulbs and observes that her pressure on the club to buy real chandeliers has been fruitless. I know where they could get them, I tell her: in the Thieves' (Chor) Bazaar.

For after going to Crawford market that first afternoon, I had drifted over to the Chor Bazaar, with its row on row of tiny shops full of the detritus of a century and a half of foreign rule. The shops are largely deserted, with the shopkeepers turning on the lights over the shelves when I arrive and turning them off when I leave. Some specialize: one, for example, in functioning Grammophones with trumpets; Italians like them, the proprietor—an albino-tells me. Some stores stock more purely functional objects: springs, or rat traps; these shops I avoid. It is the shops that are more indiscriminant that fascinate me, those with shelves upon dusty shelves of bric-a-brac left by foreigners, the siftings of a vanished civilization that have come to rest here in the backs of these shops.

Most touching for me—is it my own small children, whom I have had to leave at home to come here?—are the children's toys of a century ago, as well as the more recent ones from the 20's and 30's. The children to whom they once belonged have long since grown up; probably most of them, by now, are dead. Yet the objects that once loomed so large in their childish lives are still here in India, abandoned and left behind, both the children and their world gone, these dented toys now sold as curiosities. My feeling for these things, I think, is more than the nostalgia that grips the wanderer in the Parisian flea market at the Porte de Clingancourt; it is stronger than that, for a past more remote—almost archeological in nature, as if the objects unearth in Pompeii were to be found not in museums, but instead still in Neapolitan shops, available for purchase.

Among piles of eyeglasses and broken pen-knives are impossibly racist Victorian money boxes in the shape of torsos whose arms put pen-

nies into the mouths of bug-eyed blackamoors, who pupils loll in pleasure; there are tin push-toys of buses, Bombay to Poona they say on the
front: behind the wheel is a Sikh driver, prim British matrons in painted
profile wearing hats fill the windows, shepherding little boys such as the
ones who undoubtedly lorded it over their ayahs and terrorized the
punkha-wallah while they played with these toys. And, as I explain to my
American hostess at the club that evening, in several stores I have seen
the carefully-wrapped arms and disassembled clusters of dusty crystal
chandeliers, useless now save as grotesques. Too bad, I feel, that someone could not be deputized to go out and buy them for the club, restoring
them to something like their rightful venue.

4.

   In Hyderabad, the last of the princely states to join the Indian Union
and never part of British India, with its black-shrouded women and the
feel of the Muslim state it was, the British influence seems to have been
weakest. Outside of Hyderabad I visit the remains of Golconda, the center of a great empire that, between the 16th and 17th centuries, ruled a
region that extended north to Bengal, the source of the Kohinoor diamond as well as many other world-famous jewels, and a name still syn-
onymous in many minds both with the barbaric splendor of India, as with
vanished greatness. It was in fact destroyed by the Moghul emperor Aurangazeb, jealous of its too-great rival power to his northern Empire, not
by the British. The rulers of Golconda were Persian; so too, at far enough
remove, were the Moghuls. Who in all this were the interlopers?
   I go with an Indian friend and colleague, a professor of English literature, who is hosting me in Hyderabad. First we stop off at the stately
tombs of the kingdom's rulers, the Qutub Shas, located nearby: smaller
versions of Agra's aristocratic Taj Mahal, the real one rather than the
hotel in Bombay/Mumbai, these too are great onion domes with look-
outs and Moorish arches, mausoleums built to house tombs. Some have
been restored, with their stucco replaced. Many others are wrecks, plants
growing from their broken brickwork, dwelling places for dogs. A resto-
ration effort is underway, my friend explains, but lacks money.
   Before the largest and best-preserved of these tombs, a film is being
shot. Identically-clad chorus boys and girls in black shirts do a line dance
for the cameras while technicians set off colored smoke-bombs. My
friend tells me that all plots in contemporary Telegu films—such as this
will be—are excuses to end in a dance. From afar we see the walls and
citadel of Golconda.
   When we enter my friend is impelled to speak of Shelley's Ozyman-
dias. And indeed, it is impossible to see this great ruin save through the

eyes of the European Romantics, moved to melancholy before the signs of vanished Oriental majesty. We stand on the uppermost point, the citadel, with the remains of an open-air throne room that gives us—and gave the Shah—a view of the surrounding countryside for miles around. The corners smell of urine. Below us are the ruins of what we have been told are pleasure gardens, harems, baths. Aurangazeb wrought a pretty thorough destruction on them, I think. We descend, and find ourselves once again on the extremely bad road leading to town: the holes in the macadam, I am told, are the result of faulty contractor's work that in turn is the result of corruption. Indeed, during the night it rains and this stretch of the road is turned to a lake. The next day we must take a detour that adds half an hour to our drive between town and university.

Am I wrong to see a vestige of the splendor amid want that must have been the life of these military rulers (ultimately deposed by another, yet stronger military rules from further north), in the fact that, in this country where so many people suffer from malnutrition, the well-to-do consider it beneficial to ingest silver and gold? Pounded into breath-thin sheets of foil, it is applied to the tops of a rich toffee-like candy that is cut into elongated diamond shapes and eaten as finger food. Of *course* metals are good for the digestion, even my Western-educated friends assure me: what of copper and iron? To me, with my adolescent-era fillings, eating this candy seemed like chewing on aluminum foil, and I reached eagerly for the coffee in the airy apartment of the dance teacher where I spent the afternoon watching Bharata Natyam, the south Indian form of dancing for women that originated in the temples, and that frequently tells stories where the dancer impersonates dozens of characters, differentiating them through expression and gesture.

Out by Golconda are in fact several of the IT buildings India is so proud of in the new millennium, worlds unto themselves with gates and cars. In the center of town is an American style vertical shopping mall: the same international brands as at home are advertised. Enough NRIs, as the Indian Government calls them—Non-Resident Indians, as if to say that whatever one's passport, one remains Indian, even if not currently living there—have come back to work in the IT sector, and enough of those who never left have relatives in the States or England that both the money and the demand is there. The Indians, it's clear, are keen on anything that comes from the West, no matter how blasé we have come to feel about these things back home. Perhaps Indians will soon tire of the endless globalized brands, but for now they mean progress, modernity, and an opening to the outside world, not to mention better standards of living for a select few.

Yet another place where the British influence seems thin in the holy city of Kanchipuram, inland from Madras, perhaps thinnest of all in places like the great Vishnu temple there whose centerpiece is a mango tree. After taking off my shoes which to my find to my amazement I find, on exiting, untouched, I follow my guide along darkened hallways and before glowing statues of the god (such statues I will later see being paraded, at dusk, through choked city streets to the sound of pipes); it is cleaning time and people are vigorously throwing pails of water on dusty shrines. The water runs off black onto the floor and I am glad I have taken off my socks as well.

The idols are dressed in silks and jewels, like statues of the infant Jesus or the Virgin in French cathedrals. In a courtyard, we make the circuit of the mango tree, a gnarled giant on which are perched tiny doll's bed frames made of what seem balsa wood to which small infant-like shapes are tied. These are thanksgiving offerings, I am told, from previously barren women who have conceived after making the circuit. In another shrine, priests ask the god for his protection of me—I have told them my name is Bruce and this is repeated to the god; I receive some of the idol's flowers around my neck and a spot of sacred ash on my forehead as well as a packet of powder to take home. Then I am asked for money. The priest quickly makes clear that he wants twice what I have offered.

In a courtyard cage in this vast dark temple, we pass the huge wooden painted figures of gods and goddesses that are taken out into the streets at festival time. Now, shut away in this enclosed space like the floats from Macy's Christmas parade stored in their hangar (and just as garishly colored) their smiles seem frightening. I feel like a child lost in a world of painted toys that have swelled to nightmare proportions. I'm relieved when I emerge from the temple to watch pilgrims taking ritual baths in the great square tank, like a private geometrical lake flanked by descending steps, then look on as the tame temple elephant is put through its paces for visitors.

And then once again the Bombay airport—huge families outside milling around to bid goodbye to a single member, a snaking line of people with piles and piles of luggage, a momentary hush as a popular singer sweeps through—I have to ask who he is. Back in Germany for a day before continuing on to Washington, German friends comment on the influx since the fall of the Wall, into hitherto uniformly middle-class white German society, of Eastern Europeans and Third World people who beg on street corners. We are sitting at an outdoor café in Frankfurt near dinner time. During the course of our drinks we are serenaded by a Romanian with a harmonica who holds his cup at the end of his song, approached by a gypsy woman who wants to read our palms for a suitable hand-out, and offered flowers by a North Africa-looking girl. At a nearby fountain, three clearly German winos hold court, like the homeless men who sleep on the subway vents near the Kennedy Center in Washington where I sometimes park my car.

All is integrating, my German friends say.* We are becoming a First World in the middle of a Third World—like you in the States. Or, I add mentally, all of us in the West like India, even if not necessarily in the same proportions of poor to rich. The Indians in America are the rich ones: doctors, many of them, with easily portable skills, or the IT experts. In America the Third World is Hispanic, and walks across the border. In Europe it's Africans, who can't walk, and drown by the boatload trying to reach Spain's Canary Islands, or who jump the fence into the Spanish enclaves of Ceuta and Meilla on the North African coast.

Given the breakdown of the Wall between Western and Eastern Europe, the disappearance of the Second World, and the increasing mixture of Third into First, as Africa tries to move to Europe and Latin America to the United States, no Western country will be immune to the acrimony and divisions of the Indian political situation, its startling mixture of contrasts, of special interest groups, and of hitherto marginalized groups clambering for power. Any statistics about the widening divide between the rich and poor in America bring to mind the vast gulf between the rich and the rest in India, the precarious middle-class existence of the others. And the occasional American debate about affirmative action for the American equivalent of "Scheduled Castes" seems pale by contrast with the much more drastic strides the Indian government has taken to redress the balance of power.

In 1954, the year of my birth, Denis de Rougement (author of *Love in the Western World*) could end a meditation on a visit to India entitled "Looking for India"—one that started, like mine, at the Taj Mahal Hotel, at that time cooled only by the fans that now hang motionless from the ceiling as relics of an earlier age, and apparently staffed with many more servants bringing tea than are in fashion today—with this conclusion: "The West has problems, India *is* problems." Now, five decades later, the distinction between the two seems less clear, and the similarities more obvious.

Chapter Five
Transitions

ONE OF THE PROBLEMS THAT MUST be solved as we negotiate the boundaries between Inside and Outside, a world where it is more difficult for us to achieve the aesthetic sense of life and the one where it is much easier, is precisely that of effecting the transition. If achieving the aesthetic sense of life is a sort of quantum jump—you simply get there, or you don't—it's something of a wrench to realize that in reality, we have to negotiate this change of state. The fact of the airplane for international travel is one of the sources of problems: it's always the same, and yet we want to keep what's at the end from being part of the same world.

A meditation on this jointure, our own world to the world outside, makes clear to us as well that the world inside is riddled with potential falls down the rabbit hole, where we enter bubble worlds within—worlds we simply don't think about, given that we're so busy listening to the beat of public rhythms. The aesthetic sense of life could make us more conscious of these, and, even if we choose not to follow them up, aware that they too are part of life: the contrasts don't seem as absolute, because from the aesthetic point of view, anything is potentially able to produce a pattern—not that this is its point, merely its effect.

This realization that the world, though divided into geographic Outside and Inside, is in fact a combination of these, is what leads us to see how life with others can be lived from the aesthetic point of view: not only can the patterns of the world as experienced solo be allowed to assume the shape they are going to assume, but our relationships with others. We can be aware of the slippages between what we expect and what we get.

Most of the time, we live our lives as if we were one of the chess pieces on the board that imagine themselves in their own movement patterns, masters of their fate: if the knight failed to move two up and one over, the other pieces would be puzzled, perhaps extremely so. If the pawn suddenly moved more than a square at a time, these other pieces would undoubtedly be outraged. Occasionally, however, we become the person moving the pieces, aware of our own reactions and the fact that they are determined by what we expect to happen: were the rules we have so laboriously learned simply different, our reactions wouldn't be at all the same. This is what it means to achieve the aesthetic sense of life.

Most of our emotions of outrage, puzzlement, and hurt are produced by the sense that the world is out of joint. When we feel satisfaction, by contrast, it is because others see the same situation we see. Conflict is the result of different understandings of the lay of the land, expressed by different formulae of interaction; a sense of belonging is a result of seeing things the same way as others.

Achieving the aesthetic sense of life doesn't mean we don't feel these things, the things that we feel as a chess piece on the board. It means feeling them—but simultaneously being aware of how they fit into the larger scheme of things, being aware of ourselves as the outraged or satisfied chess piece, laughing tolerantly at the fact that we are condemned to have this reaction, as others are condemned to have theirs.

Too fast

Nostalgia for ocean liners seems a thing of the past. Certainly ships are no viable alternatives to getting places, so that we can buffer the transposition to Europe with a week of doing other things, killing time in luxury. Instead, we find ourselves brutally changed from one place to another via the airplane. And ships being so long ago in our collective memory, we can no longer even compare the abrupt airplane transposition with its predecessor from the 1930s and 1940s. We no longer long for the slow trip via the Cunard to Europe, during which—as people said with a sigh for a decade or two after the rise to prominence of the airplane, which for a time had its own chic, travel with gloves and hat, and the aura of the "jet set"—"one at least could get used to the idea of another country." The getting used to, if it happens, has to happen quickly: there's no alternative.

Still, many of us, even without a viable alternative to contrast with the mass-market no-frills airplane travel of the present day, do have the sense that planes—our current default transportation medium—are simply too fast. Too fast for what, we can no longer say; too fast compared to what is no longer a comparison we can fill in. But still we sense the too fast, even without having a concrete contrast definer to anchor our reactions. Now we arrive in Paris with the food from Washington still in our intestines, drag ourselves into our hotel room in Bombay to awake the next morning to the foetid air of the Arabian Sea after the early spring of the American East Coast. The girl behind the desk in her sari works here every day, certainly boards a crowded commuter train from the far-flung suburbs and changes into her sari once she gets here. The taximan who waits upon us is anxious to get many fares to feed his family; he asks us where we are going the next day. The ferry operator out to Elephanta Island runs this route several times a day. But their world is not our world; we are here for something else, and we cannot enter into the pattern of their lives.

Suddenly we are in a world where we do not have to catch the train into town, or the next vaporetto, if we are Italian, or the U-Bahn, if German or Austrian: we have other givens, but not those. Or perhaps we have no givens at all; we're on vacation—which means precisely, have slipped the cogs of the patterns that otherwise define our existence. We see the people hurrying to fulfill the givens of their world—their taxis, their jobs, their ferries, and look at them with curiosity, from afar. It's as if we see the cogs, if at all, from a position where we ourselves are not one of them: we note a complex machine, or accept that it has to be such, if only we were willing to take the time to figure it out. But it is not our machine; it seems curious, not vital.

And yet if we stay more than a few days we begin to adapt, not only to the diurnal rhythms, but to the fact that for the locals, this world—to us so alien, so quaint—is quite real, the struggles real struggles, not pretend ones, the rents real rent, not daily ones in a hotel, the givens real givens. And so many times we are glad to go, feeling once again clinging to us the sense that we have to get up and go, enter the rat race of these particular rats, be something other than a tourist or a visiting businessman, but a local. As a result this sense of slipping cogs even works, quite as abruptly, when we return home—for in the time spent away our body clocks, like those of our sleep cycles, have begun to re-adjust to the point where the things that seem important to the locals have, in diluted form, begun to seem important to us as well, as if our bodies, used to responding to the marching cadence of our own life had, after a period of relief at the absence of any regularity at all, begun to seek the insistent boom-boom that gives rhythm to existence and had borrowed someone else's.

When we return home, there is a brief echo of a second-order vacation when the fainter regularities we had begun to assume, *faute de mieux* and in need of some pattern to our existence, when we feel the pattern we had begun to assume draining from us. We awake the next morning, when perhaps we have scheduled nothing, or find ourselves on a weekend that seems even more delicious than usual because we shed so easily the pale pattern of our borrowed lives that had hardly begun to penetrate below the surface and have not yet reconciled ourselves to the fact that shortly we will resume the pattern it had, if only briefly, replaced. The birds sing outside, we roll over in bed again as the light streams in the window and the cat (cared for by the sitter during our absence) stretches herself in the sun.

Both coming and going, the shock is abrupt—in the way that makes us postulate a now-absent comparison—more abrupt than what? Well, since we can't reach for ocean liners to make our comparison: more abrupt that it should be. How, we wonder, is it possible for such different parallel existences to go on, these two different cadences where, at least for a few days on each end, the one has not yet completely disappeared, so that the result is like a John Cage piece for multiple radios set to different stations, or a Charles Ives cacophony. And then we realize with a shudder that we have only two to compare: we have just come from, say, Venice, or Vienna, or Vladivostock—from only one of these, that is; not from all three. It's not anywhere near the screaming polyphony of Ives or Cage; the voices that compete in our heads are only two.

World of the happy man

Yet we may reflect that not all parallel, but disjunctive, existences are to be found at the other end of an airplane ride. We think: how many parallel existences are there right in our own hometown? The differences between lives are not merely geographical or cultural: they can be personal too. Though economics will mandate similarity to some degree between the people who live in one area, part of town, or apartment building, what of those in another section? What of the fact, as Wittgenstein has it, that "the world of the happy man is a different one than the world of the unhappy man"? That two people in contiguous apartments, sharing a wall that transmits versions however muffled and blurred of their comings and goings, music and parties, can live in different worlds, one the world of the happy, another the world of the unhappy?

But most of us balk at that kind of thinking. This kind of world, the next door "world of the (un)happy (wo)man kind," is not something we can walk into. And there are simply too many of them for us to be able to afford to even pay attention to them. This kind of thinking leads to eye-rolling at best and instantaneous burn-out at worst: it's the metaphysical equivalent of what charity organizations call "donor fatigue." You can't give to everybody. Though the milk of human kindness may flow at the first hard-luck story, probably also at the second, and then even possibly the third, it quickly dries up: one horror scenario is as bad as the next, the whole the anesthetized war pictures of 1960s television. You can simply turn down the volume, or turn off the television, and go back to eating Cheese Crispies and re-arranging the knick-knacks. We know it's true that each person's world is his or her own, but we can't afford to let this knowledge really affect us. There are simply too many individuals in the world. Yet there aren't too many exotic places—not more than a handful that we Westerners are working at any one time, in fact. Those on the borders aren't exotic, they just don't figure on the map.

That's why it's so salutary going to a different place—the problem being, we don't know where "different" is to be found. Across the world to a place just like home may not be enough to qualify for "different," but different may in fact be in an enclave at the end of the road. Usually the fact of another language, another cuisine, and another set of givens for getting through the day will be enough to give us a breather from our own life. But distance too usually helps, though it guarantees nothing. What we need is a sense of distance, which helps us create or be aware of (the difference is ultimately irrelevant) another world: if it's only across town, we're unlikely to be able to build around it the mental barriers necessary to us not feeling the drag of our daily habits. It's 9, I have to be doing such-and-so: this is what we think at the end of the road. When we go to another place, however, we think: it's not 9 here, and I have no control over life back home.

If we make this jump too quickly, the result is momentary vertigo, a version of those data-confusion moment where we are simultaneously high in a building and falling to the spot we are looking at, hearing one thing and having to ignore it for something else, seeing something for the first time and feeling its inevitability as a déjà vu (caused, scientists tell us, by a perception being mis-routed through the brain's memory circuits), or feeling our heart simultaneously in our body and having dropped the six floors the elevator has abruptly descended. It's too fast; we straddle a divide opening wider between our feet, two parts of the earth's crust dividing and leaving us neither on one nor on the other, in danger of falling into the abyss.

Tectonic plates

It's moments like this when we're aware of the multiple tectonic plates into which the world divides—moments when we're caught, if only briefly, between them. And it's at moments like this that we think the transition too quick, too abrupt. In the case of airplane travel, the new is thrust upon us, we don't seek it—and until we become at one with the feeling of it being there, it feels like an intrusion. Yet this too is something the aesthetic sense of life can help us with: what we articulate is precisely this.

The jolt is particularly intense when we fit such a new world into our own for only a few days, and do so without radically disrupting our schedule. We go away for a long week-end to another place, another continent—and find on returning home that our houseplants have not even wilted, the tropical fish have nibbled on a special white vacation food that dissolves slowly, and we haven't been missed. In this sudden crack we have, however, inserted a whole new world: between, as it were, two bats of an eyelash, we have traveled to the moon and returned to Earth.

We have, for example, inserted into our brick apartment in Chicago the world of a Moroccan city, complete with heat, dust, veiled women, camels, and the vestiges of the French—and in this time the leftovers in the refrigerator have not even grown mold, and we eat the remains of the chicken breasts we served to the neighbors the night before we left for the airport. Or we have changed climate zones, packing another hemisphere's and another season's clothing inserted into our northern winter, or more onerously, the reverse, re-entering boots and woolens we had consigned to the furthest closet, suddenly bitten with cold of a Patagonian winter when at home we lounged in shorts.

Successfully inserting such worlds into the normal rhythm of our lives—between two successive weekly whatevers (trips to the grocery store, waterings of plants, appointments with our personal trainer) that we come back to find somehow unaltered by the entire world we have inserted into the crack—makes us realize that most of what we think we perceive in life is not really perceived, but filled in, in the manner of our eye's blind spot. We are most aware of our biological blind spot when we turn our head in the car and suddenly find a vehicle barreling up our left side, having appeared it seems from nowhere. If our blind spot is centered over the one fault in the perfect geometrical pattern we would swear that there is no flaw.

Perceptually this means, the patterns that determine our lives generate heads of steam of their own. They keep on moving at their own speed and straight ahead, unaware (if we may personify them) that the ground may momentarily not be there to support them. We insert a few days in Marrakesh into our lives in New York and find it somehow odd that the man who hands out the towels at our club greets us as if he didn't even know we'd been away—as in fact he doesn't; we're not changed in the interim. He assumes we've continued on in the same pattern—or rather, this being his blind spot, doesn't ask. Reflections on all these slippages is something the aesthetic sense of life can offer us.

Double lives

The fact that others assume we're merely filling time in the usual way between sightings must, we reflect, be what's behind those stories we occasionally come across, perhaps more in the late Victorian age—

what historians call the "long nineteenth century," that lasted until World War I—of bigamists, people who, like the father of J. R. Akerley (*My Father and Myself*) were discovered after his death to have had a common-law wife and several by then grown or almost-grown children in a suburban semi-detached villa, all of whom somehow have to be accommodated by the will or whose mere existence is revealed by a sealed letter marked, in large emphatic letters, NOT TO BE OPENED BEFORE MY DEATH. In the era of fewer questions, more respect (or so it was labeled) for the *pater familias*, the husband could simply announce he was going "away" and insert into one existence the other, as if between two ends of the lifetime of the leftovers in the refrigerator—put in fresh on leaving and eaten just before the first hint of rottenness upon returning, so that it seemed that no time at all had passed.

Back then, it seems, this kind of double existence was possible. But it makes this world itself seem an alien one to us. What a different world than ours seems the world of Sherlock Holmes's "Twisted Man" Adventure—where the wife knows only of her husband's business that he does "something" in the City. Her background and presuppositions fill in the blind spot, making her assume that her husband is merely one among the hoards of top-hatted businessmen whom T. S. Eliot, in a later time, saw streaming across London Bridge, undone by death. In fact this particular husband dons a disfiguring disguise and begs for change on a street corner—something neither her world nor his would make probable: it's explained to us when all is clear that initially the idea was part of a newspaper article he, a reporter, was writing. It was only when the piece was turned in and he found himself low on cash that he realized the money he had gotten from passers-by as part of his disguise was something he could continue to get again, this time as an end in itself.

Indeed most Sherlock Holmes stories turn on double lives, things out of the ordinary, the presupposition being that life in the metropolis and the home country is pretty faded, regulated, and law-abiding: all these murders turn out to be revenge for something done in the uncivilized world outside—Australia, then deepest bush, or India, or America, the land of the cowboys. In the interim the young men have grown old and gray, but retribution for a youthful betrayal comes to them at last. Sherlock Holmes knows that the world outside is a dangerous one, and that the man who is apparently a law-abiding squire in Somerset may in his youth have been a train robber, a gold miner, or an adventurer in the wilds of the outback.

Why does this sort of lurid past in the Wild Wild West seem so old-fashioned to us now? Perhaps we simply don't leave the metropolis in our youth the way young men did in the age of Empire. Or we presuppose a greater degree of knowledge of those we live—perhaps we pre-suppose too much, more than we should. The idea of a contemporary wife being satisfied with a vague idea of "business in the City" to answer what her husband does, as in "The Adventure of the Twisted Man," is ludicrous. Perhaps not so ludicrous is the game played by Severine, the heroine of Joseph Kessel's novel *Belle de Jour*, better known as the source of Buñuel's film by the same name—where Catherine Deneuve's glacial beauty is contrasted to good effect with the tawdry sexual escapades she undergoes as a daytime call-girl. Her husband assumes she merely amuses herself in the manner of other women of her class; in fact she fits into these parameters—disappearing in the morning, reappearing in the late afternoon to preside over her house—another life, a flower that blooms every day anew, as the title suggests. Or even this may nowadays be untenable, where domestic partners of a certain class assume they know at least something beyond the grossest outlines of the other's life.

Emma

We might say, it seems unforgivable to deceive a spouse. More to the point, fatiguing. It might seem clever to figure out the things the person most intimate with us won't suspect, the blind spots in our relationship. But we all have to presuppose something: no relationship is without blind spots, even if they're probably smaller in absolute size than those we presuppose with the checker in the supermarket, a waiter in a restaurant. Of course we can figure out what this person takes for granted and do something different with this: perhaps it's the time we're supposed to be going to work, or running errands. It's of course possible to do something different with this time, though we have to be careful that we can make the insertions seamless and that the world we're inserting into the cracks doesn't intrude into the other one.

In Flaubert's *Madame Bovary*, the adulterous wife, Emma, is carrying on an affair in the city with a young man she had met as part of her family circle, who by this point has moved away. She inserts the affair into her normal life by ostensibly taking piano lessons, something she has gotten her slow-witted husband himself to agree to, indeed positively encourage, after a scene where she banged the top of the piano and complained of how out of practice she was getting. Once a week she goes to town to "take piano lessons"—inserting another life into hers at home.

Flaubert too is interested in the phenomenon of the blind spots of relationships; he goes out of his way to make Charles, the husband, even blinder than most men, less suspecting of anything going on than a normal man would be. The fact that Emma fills the spots is partly due to the fact that there are so many of them to fill, and that they are such large ones. To begin with, any mildly observant husband would realize that what Charles is doing for his wife sexually is not going to be enough to satisfy her: Flaubert makes sure we understand that Charles's lovemaking is on a clock, quickly finished, always the same, and rare. He's set up a situation where it would be particularly difficult for a woman not to look for ways to fill the blind spots with an alternative life—and Emma is a woman who is always dreaming of the exotic. The disaster of their collective life is an inevitable smash-up produced as much by the one as by the other.

Flaubert engineers a situation akin to the child's theater where the children in the audience are shouting at the actors the solution to the puzzle—where the clown is hidden, for example—and the actors pretend not to understand, which only makes the children holler louder, with greater frustration but with greater glee. Flaubert loves situations where the audience is in on the joke and Charles is not: when Emma's first lover, Rodolphe, finally can take no more of her airs and antics and has no intention of fulfilling her demands that he sweep her away to live in Italy (he's a wealthy landowner; Emma is merely one in a long line of mistresses and he's tiring of her anyway), he writes her a kiss-off letter and leaves the neighborhood. He has the letter delivered to her in a basket of fruit which he's ostensibly sending to both Emma and Charles; Emma sees the letter in the fruit, reads it without Charles seeing, and faints as Charles continues to press on her the ripe peaches from the basket. In the background she hears Rodolphe's coach rumbling away and realizes her hopes have been shattered. How clueless can Charles be? we wonder.

Completely clueless, it seems: the reader assumes Emma's "piano lessons" are over when Charles, for once himself in the city, meets none other than Emma's piano teacher, whom he knows. He asks how Emma is doing, is told she has showed up for only a few lessons and not for a long time, and repeats this to Emma. Emma, quick-witted as always, assures him that the teacher has so many pupils she can't remember them all, and produces a sheaf of receipts for lessons taken that has "fallen in a shoe." It's a given that Flaubert will have Charles fall for this; any premature stop to the insertions sooner than the great crash planned for the end would destroy the delicious frustration of the audience: No! we want to cry at Charles. Don't believe it! Don't do it! But Charles continues as if in a dream or another dimension, oblivious of the audience.

This constitutes deception; Emma is, as we say, cheating on Charles. He continues to fill in the blind spots where she is inserting another life, as if she had gone for the weekend to Istanbul, seen people oblivious to her ordinary life, and of whom she herself is oblivious. But this situation is different only in degree rather than kind from the way we work with others to keep the pattern the same for them: we always tell co-workers that we are "fine" even when we aren't simply because we want to keep the pattern going and not make them deal with diversions. Things have to cross a magic line of bad before they register in such an interchange.

Similarly, we can keep from our closest friend, even our spouse, things below a certain line of seriousness—perhaps even beyond them. If they see no evidence that we're unwell, for example, they'll continue to assume we're well—sometimes precisely that is what we intend. In John Galsworthy's *Forsyth Saga*, the painter Julian Forsyth keeps his impending death from his wife, confessing only to his daughter. This too may seem somewhat dated, and indeed one of the qualities of our modern age is the urge to share even the smallest thing with perfect strangers.

Wandern

When I lived in Germany I went on Saturday hikes (*"Wandern gehen"*) with older colleagues of the family on the upper floor of whose house I lived, all of them professors at the university where I had a lower position. They were pleasant, and I got along with them well in a formal way, our verbal exchanges couched in the professional formal "you" (Sie) still standard among Germans of a certain generation. Indeed the relationship between the two sets of professors and their families were also couched in the "Sie" form, though they had been friends, after a fashion, for decades.

I then went away and, for two years, discovered what for me was another world: central Africa. Returning from there to visit, I was invited once again, on a Saturday, to go once more hiking with Kesslers. I didn't want to talk about all I'd seen without being asked, but I thought it odd that they asked me nothing but how I was—Wie geht's Ihnen, Herr Fleming—as if I had merely left them to go to the corner. They asked nothing of the strange world I had discovered. But, I reflected, correcting myself: for that matter it had been there all along; the newness was merely my discovery. Perhaps I was the one who had to get used to the idea that it had been carrying out its life even in my absence.

Checkout line

How many such cracks can be opened up in life? With chance acquaintances, so many it's not even interesting to think about them. We can go away to another country, another continent, and they hardly register the fact. How would we gracefully tell the man handing out towels in the gym that since we saw him last (we could easily miss several weeks, if not months, without his remarking: he's not there all the time either, and has substitutes, or we could have come at different times) that we've done such and so during the time in which he didn't see us? It would be pushy, and appropriate only if he wanted to chat. Then we'd have to downplay things: Yeah, I've been on business in Tokyo. Come to think of it, in Argentina too. (We probably wouldn't say Buenos Aires unless we had reason to think him a tad more sophisticated than most fellows who hand out towels in gyms.) And he'd say, "Awesome, dude," and we'd take the towel and say "thanks." And that would be that.

Or the checkout cashier in the supermarket which employs dozens. Perhaps over a decade we would find ourselves in one particular person's line several times a year: over a decade, it's enough to make a pattern. But the pattern can be interrupted for six months without causing any notice. One year, a chatty checker told me a story about a customer who arrived at her counter finishing up the mouthful of peanuts he'd just polished off, and whose cost, of course, would be factored into the breakages and petty thievery that would be passed on to other customers. It had come up naturally, in connection with my having started a gallon of milk in the store—she was afraid it was leaking; I reassured her, and noted that food in stores divided into the two categories of those that could be started on, those sold as a package whose price didn't vary after sampling, and those that couldn't, those sold by weight or number. For the next five years, until I left the neighborhood, that story was our point of reference.

I could have done practically anything in the time between meetings with this woman and had her react in the same way; the time scale governing our interactions was such that the only thing that might have justifiably answered a casual enquiry about "How have you been?" would have been something on the order of "We bought a new house." Or perhaps the other extreme, the day before: "Well, I've got a little cold, but I guess it's the season." Not: "I've had a child and gotten a divorce and published a book since I saw you last." The jolt is simply too extreme.

And the reverse: this woman may have gone through momentous changes herself, but as long as she has the same three earrings in her left ear and is at the same register, or nearby, we can pick up where we left off with the peanuts. I assume that her life has moved along in its usual paths as well. Perhaps she too has been left by a husband, or left one, or gotten married, or had a child. If I saw her every few months, she might mention she was getting married, or had, or I would notice her pregnancy. These are predictable milestones. It would even be possible for her, or me, to die between visits: death is always abrupt.

Autism

One of the tests for possible autism in small children involves explaining a situation where one child, call her Sally, hides an object. She leaves, and Nelly (say) enters, finds the object, and puts it in another place. The child being tested is then asked, Where will Sally look for the object when she in turn re-enters the room? The child with a tendency to autism, knowing from the story where the object in fact is (where Nelly has put it), will answer from what he or she now knows, saying that Sally will look for it where Nelly has put it. The sign of autism is that we fail to realize another, here Sally, doesn't know what we ourselves know.

When I first took my daughter, at that point recently diagnosed with mild autism, to meet her new Kindergarten teacher, we took a book of Disney World photographs as a conversation starter. Alexandra showed her new teacher the pictures of her dancing along in the Main Street Parade. The teacher said, "I've been there too."

"No," said Alexandra. And later the teacher told me she had Alexandra's number (as we say, to indicate that someone has understood another person) in that moment: Alexandra hadn't seen her there when she herself was there, so for Alexandra, the teacher had never been there.

Yet all of us tend to this form of autism, and have to be talked out of it, acknowledging ruefully that others have lives too that we don't control and can't predict. We assume that things go on in the direction they always have done, and that what we know, others must know too. I remember the feeling of almost guilt I had when I visited our favorite Vietnamese restaurant in our old neighborhood. Though the time that had elapsed since my last visit was not exponentially longer than the time between some other visits when I still lived in that neighborhood, I felt I was coming under false pretenses, as if I were leading on the kindly waiter who had always made so much of my daughter. I knew I no longer lived in this neighborhood, and somehow assumed he must know this too.

In fact, I could continue to visit just as frequently as before, or so nearly that the alteration of pattern would not be noticed—he needn't know anything at all about where I lived, that now I had to drive across town and make a special trip to do something that before had been routine. Yet I somehow felt the need to explain it to him, until I caught myself, and laughing at my silliness, reminded myself that he didn't care where I lived or how far I had to drive to come here. What before had been part of the rhythm of my life could still be kept up as a pattern, albeit now an alien one.

Crime novels are full of such patterns created knowingly: we can imagine someone who set up the pattern of visiting this Vietnamese restaurant under the pretense of living in the neighborhood in order to establish an alibi, like the Victorian husband who appeared at the suburban semi-detached housing his "other" family as the kindly Uncle Horace, off again all too soon on business. They work within the presuppositions of people's worlds: if we come often to this one restaurant, the natural assumption will be that we live in the neighborhood. It might turn out we have a reason for coming here: a family member, say, or a recurring appointment. But why otherwise would someone from the other side of the city come to this particular spot? It's possible, but it's not likely. And we assume the likely until given reason not to.

Playing with trust

We're not always aware of what we assume, in fact rarely so unless it's challenged. One long airplane ride I saw fragments of a program from Canadian television program was clearly meant to be humorous, a series of situations where actors did strange things and the camera recorded people's reactions: to me they were all merely designed to show what in fact we take for granted. One sequence consisted of a person hung upside-down from a crane suddenly appearing headfirst outside the window of a motorist at a red light. The viewers were meant to find amusing the driver's reaction of fright followed by nervous laughter, hand to chest, and so on—their shock at seeing something so improbable. Another skit involved a woman in a floppy hat accosting passing males to cry on their chests. She cried and cried; the men were disconcerted, caught between annoyance and chivalry, tentative pats combining with puzzled faces. Another skit involved a man who'd ask someone to pick up an object and then throw it down again. The person accosted would frequently think s/he had misunderstood the situation, and pick it up again, only to have it thrown down again.

These merely seemed predictable to me, proof that people have a developed sense of the norm. A woman in tears in a public place is usually in some sort of major trouble, not an actress. If someone wants our help picking something up, we are trained to help. The upside down person is startling in a way another car pulling up beside us isn't: we're expecting the other car, or at least aren't surprised. We don't expect the upside-down person. Indeed, if such camera skits were frequently done, we'd immediately assume, on seeing an upside-down person, that we were on TV. And any future show would have to find something strange in this new world to exploit.

A book of operatic gaffes and humor I read contained the story of a repeated prank by a famous conductor, an eminent and gray-haired man. He'd turn to his dinner companion, invariably a lissome woman (tables were arranged male/female/male/female—and he'd have been given an attractive female) and invite her to "feel the heat emanating from these mashed potatoes." When, somewhat puzzled, she'd extend her hand, he'd ram it into the potatoes. Ba-da-boom. Who expects a serious elderly gentleman to do such a thing? But there are a thousand unexpected things he might do at dinner: take off his clothes, begin to sing, declaim at the top of his voice, dance on the table, and so on. In the same way, my study could have been booby-trapped so that the keys to the computer each did something I didn't expect (I merely expect the "e" to produce and "e" on the screen, and so on), the light to spit sparks when I turn it on, the chair to spin around of its own accord, and so ad infinitum. In the same way we can booby-trap the world into the child's book *Wacky Wednesday*, where on every page many impossible things are afoot.

The only reason we'd get a response is that we've learned that things simply aren't this way, at least not most of the time: we are filling in the blind spot, and have never seriously thought about the fact that we're doing so. If the computer key "e" made an "e" the last time, the time before, and moreover is designed to make an "e," we'll be surprised if it makes a "b" instead. If that's the only thing wrong we're likely to blame mechanical error. But if everything is wrong, and we can think of a reason—workmen were in the house, the computer is a cheap one about which we've heard bad things, we know we're being bugged by the FBI—we begin to look for explanations, as Charles Bovary might have looked for explanations of why the piano teacher his wife had purportedly been seeing once a week for some time didn't even remember seeing her. (Part of the joke is that Charles clearly can't put himself in the position of the piano teacher: of course she'd remember each pupil, no matter how many she had. Charles evidently believes she wouldn't.)

It's not at all funny to see people shocked or puzzled when things don't work the way they usually do: the joke is simply potentially too ubiquitous. Anybody who puts his or her mind to it can think of a thousand ways to make things be different than they typically are. Individually, these go nowhere: the weeping woman in the television show was merely an actress, the upside down person suspended from a crane. Once over our momentary shock and puzzlement we go our way, wiser the next time in all probability.

In the hands of someone with an agenda, however, consciousness of the fact that others are filling in their blind spots can be a way to manipulate others: the cheating spouse is the classic example. So too the elaborate set-up of the movie "The Sting," where a gambling den was set up for the sole purpose of getting money from the mark, with an elaborate apparent double-cross scheme that would make him flee and not look back. Who would ever be so self-centered as to think that things apparently just here in the world were in fact put here for one's self?

The Lady Vanishes

In Hitchcock's movie "The Lady Vanishes" the heroine, a spunky young woman who insists that her companion, an elderly lady with whom she boarded the train in some politically unstable Eastern European or Balkan *pays d'operette*, had in fact been kidnapped—everyone else on the train insists she was never there—finally comes to realize that the whole train is in cahoots, or is going along with the lie for a reason that coincidentally supports the story of those who are in cahoots (two possibly gay cricket-mad Englishmen support the assertion that Miss Froy, the companion, was never there simply because they're afraid if they acknowledge a kidnapping they won't be back in time for their cricket match). The turning point comes when the heroine realizes that a nun apparently guarding an invalid swathed in bandages is wearing high heels under her head-to-toe habit. From this she concludes correctly that the woman isn't a nun, and surmises, also correctly, that the invalid is in fact her Miss Froy. It's possible to arrive at the conclusion that what seems merely to be there as brute reality is in fact calculated to produce effects in one's self: it's like deciding that the so-called "pathetic fallacy," whereby nature is held to mirror our moods, is in fact quite correct. Stories like that of "The Sting" or "The Lady Vanishes," or a later and lesser work after Agatha Christie, "Murder on the Orient Express," turn out to be such hugely enjoyable riddles where what seems objective in fact is all about appearing objective to someone, much as the cheating spouse laboriously creates the illusion of normalcy in the hopes of not being discovered.

The aesthetic sense involves awareness of the transitions and slippages between the structures we take for granted and those we don't, the inevitable alterations produced by the fact of our blind spots.

Chapter Six
Science, Religion, and the Aesthetic Sense

BECAUSE THE EXTREMELY WORLDLY focus on individual details and allow only their personal "choice" to explain how they get from one to another, they fill in the area beyond what they perceive and know with a single concept that itself is not amenable to questioning, "belief."

Consider a conversation I had with a former student of mine, now a young officer in the Marine Corps. I had some credibility with him, both as his former professor and as a fellow weight room user, where the conversation took place. So I felt I could make a comment about the brick-red color, obviously the result of too much sun that weekend, of his normally beige face. "Slather on that sun block," I encouraged him. To avoid any appearance of telling him what to do—after all, I'm not in his chain of command now—I immediately added, "My mother has to go to the dermatologist every year or so to get stuff cut off her face. And she never really even went in the sun."

The young man's response was interesting. "I believe," he said, "that heredity has as much to do with whether you get that stuff as going out in the sun." The officer was telling me what he believed. Immediately I had a thousand questions, reasons why the state of affairs he was suggesting might well be false, and in any case why it could not be asserted without substantiation. He was offering me belief; my impulse was to respond with analysis. But the aesthetic sense includes an appreciation of both, and a realization that they interlock hand-in-glove.

Analysis is in the middle of the scale on which the worldly is at one end, the religious at the other. Like the aesthetic sense of life, to which it bears some similarity as it does to the scientific viewpoint, it presupposes an openness to the world: we don't know what we're going to find until we look. It may be that the scientific is not typically found in the same person as the aesthetic, narrowly understood (though it's not unknown: physicists who play the flute or violin are more than a small handful)—but the two attitudes toward the world have at least this in common. Perhaps for this reason the "arts and sciences," together, comprise the "liberal arts"—all of them are in the middle of the same scale. So here, "belief" indicates that a person is neither seeing the world from an aesthetic point of view, nor a scientific one.

The distinction between belief and analysis is between two fundamental manners of doing things: it's the dichotomy played out in the ongoing public discussion between matters of faith and matters of science. Currently this discussion is couched in terms of a conflict between teaching what the Hebrew Bible is held to say about the creation of the world, and teaching what science, building on Darwin, says on the same subject. It's not a new conflict—it's been stalemated since the Victorian age—but political trends events in America have made it topical again. (For a more extended discussion of our culture wars see my *Why Liberals and Conservatives Clash*.) Parents demand that "Creation Science" be given equal billing with Evolution in science classes, or that "Intelligent Design" be taught as an explanation for the nature of the universe; judges disagree, and the cycle starts again. Centuries ago, for that matter, the Catholic Church demanded that Galileo recant: science has been challenging faith for centuries. And theologians have been trying to figure out the relationship between faith and reason for millennia.

Not that analysis is even always an option: here in the weight room it wasn't—both of us were sweating, and there was no way we were about to have a philosophical discussion in the middle of the workout. (It's not by chance that the Socratic dialogues when men are simply sitting around with nothing to do but talk.) I could explain what was happening, but could not adjourn the conversation to go to the talk laboratory. Besides, by running this young man's casual remark to earth I was attempting to re-establish the professorial power position, something I had no chance of pulling off with an almost-30-year old US Marine, especially if it was being re-asserted out of the blue, in an "off time" place like the weight room. (It could be re-established, if he willingly signed up for my class, just the way if you ask to be in a boxing class you expect that somebody will be taking a swing at you. You don't like it if somebody takes a swing at you out of nowhere, and you're as outraged that it happened when you didn't expect it as by the swing itself.) More fundamental still, the natural medium of male-male verbal interaction, especially when something physical is involved, is grunts, not extensive talk, such as this required. I could process this situation only using the aesthetic sense of life. Yet though the words tasted dry in my brain as I geared up to utter them, and were even drier as they came out of my mouth, I did try to object to my Marine's assertion of belief. After all, I was here, a part of this situation: I was inside it, reacting to my own position in the world. This is what I take to be definitory of the aesthetic sense of life, here opposed to his "belief."

"You mean, equal amount of influence?" I asked. "Why equal?"

He didn't see where my question was coming from, but saw he had to explain his response. "My father worked all his life in the sun and never had problems," he said.

I began to object then gave up: "Here I am turning into a professor again," I said. "Well, gotta get back to lifting."

I couldn't interact with him; I could only process the world of which I was a part by musing on it to myself, from the perspective of the aesthetic. Here's what I couldn't say, the analysis I wanted to offer in place of his "belief." He was citing a single case as the basis for his conclusion, namely his father. What can be concluded from a single case? Is it typical? Is it even statistically significant? Even given the fact that his father didn't get skin cancer despite years in the sun, why would he assume that the reason for this was heredity, rather than something else? Is "heredity" here functioning as a general label for "all other factors"? If so, why call it this? Surely the term "heredity" implies not only protection for the father, but also for the son, so it was suspiciously convenient for the Captain to argue that he needn't bother with sunblock, or even to stay out of the sun. Even if heredity did in fact play a role, how could my Marine say that it played an "equal" role with sun exposure? Why 50% influence? Why not 20%? Why not say we don't know the exact percentage?

What of his more basic assumption still, namely that the "I believe" button was there to be pushed at all so close to the point where his personal knowledge ran out? That if he didn't know something, he could legitimately fill in the blank with "belief" at all rather than simply saying he didn't know? Clearly he thought he could. For me, leaving a blank of "I don't know; maybe others do" is a legitimate way to proceed. Is this in turn merely my own "belief" that counters his "belief"? Or is it something of a higher order?

Asking for justification, or being willing to listen to it—the game I wanted to play but couldn't—is to presuppose the game of interaction with another person isn't over. It's the quintessential scientific response. The nature of "belief," by contrast, is to declare the game is over. There's no way to negotiate with someone who doesn't want to continue the game. Negotiating is precisely the game they're no longer willing to play. Such people aren't interacting with the world; they're applying a formula to it.

The person who wanted to continue to discuss, here me, would probably say not just "discuss" but "discuss rationally," as if achieving belief were not a rational act. So let's ask: Is it irrational to turn off the machinery of what we call "rationality," the apparatus of evidence and proof that is the mainstay of the scientific enterprise? There's no way to get both sides to agree on the answer to this. Moving outside a specific way of doing things is always something adherents of that way will resist, and something an external viewpoint can do quite easily. That, after all, is what it means to be outside. "You can't do that!" the one interested in continuing the conversation rationally will insist. "Watch me," says the believer, as s/he walks away.

A person can live with his or her finger pressed down all the time on the "I believe" button. We can "believe" that our breakfast cereal turns to Kryptonite when we eat it, that if we walk in front of cars we will not be killed, and that God cares if our team wins the Big Game. The arguments against beginning belief at any given point are always offered from the point of view of the person opposing belief, or more usually, opposed to pressing the "I believe" button *at that point.* They'll try to (as they'd say) warn us: you'll get run over, cereal is cereal and anyway Kryptonite isn't real, and God doesn't care whether your team wins: what do you say when you lose? Negative experiences (say, being run over) can cause us to revise the point at which we push the "I believe" button. But they need not cause us to call into question the act of pressing it.

When, not whether

Most conflicts arise not over whether it's *ever* legitimate to press the "I believe" button, but over whether it should be done right here, right now. Even scientists agree people may press the "I believe" button when they reach the outside of our most current available explanation. Yet typically the same scientists are firmly opposed to people pushing the button at earlier points, such as the point of "we will win this football game because God is on our side." They want the space cleared for what they do; those who press the "I believe" button much earlier aren't so concerned to clear that space.

To me, it seemed that my Marine had pushed the "I believe" button too soon, and that his pushing doing so was something that needed to be justified. And so I raised objections, realizing (this the aesthetic sense) that there was little likelihood I could convince him of my point of view—more to the point, that I wouldn't even be allowed, and this by the situation itself, to try.

Still, the most startling quality of what I heard was that apparently, for this young man, the boundary of belief began at the edge of the immediately known. This is the earliest possible place that belief can begin, but the decision to let it begin here is not one that belief itself can legislate. Deciding when to cross the line into the territory of belief is like walking a narrow path on the edge of the cliff: we can step off at any point. What's up for grabs is whether we do so earlier or later, or at all. But at whatever point we do it, assuming we do, the step off feels the same.

What does belief have going for it?

It's clear why people are drawn to belief. It stops the game of interaction with others, those others asking you to justify, generalize, distance yourself, test. And that means, others cease to matter; you believe what you believe. The defining quality of "belief" is that it's something completely within the power of the single person. In this it's like the "choice" that provides the glue for the specifics of the world for what is usually the same group of people.

Religion isn't the only complex of ideas to invoke belief but it's one of the most developed. Other people don't enter into the equation, save tangentially. That's why the ends of the spectrum in which the aesthetic sense of life and the scientific point of view are in the center may bear resemblance to each other, at least in vocabulary. Religion is typically all about *my* purity or salvation, not that of others. Thus religion would be foolish to allow too much of the scientific viewpoint to enter into it, which insists that people can't ever get their beliefs and hang onto them: they have to constantly subject them to questions.

People operating on the basis of beliefs can, of course, interact with others regarding their beliefs. We can explain why we push the "I believe" button, and when. But pushing the button itself, once it's pushed, is not something that need be, or can be, justified: justification comes before pushing the button, not after. The person who steps off the edge can only be reasoned with before, not after. Reason is the language of the solid land, which is to say, of other people.

Proof

Sometimes we confuse the scientific viewpoint with a demand for proof, as if no one but scientific types understood the notion of proof. But what's scientific about this is not the way of thinking, it's the size of the net cast for possible disproof. In scientific thinking, the net is much larger, possibly infinite. This makes certainty difficult, and qualified. Everyone understands disproof, but people who frequently invoke "belief" tend to understand disproof as being based on things they're already aware of. What's in the corral is what's in the corral; that's what you deal with. In science, people are always scouting for new things in the corral. That makes it difficult to wrap things up. Scientific thinking asks us to go out of our way to subject what we say to the withering fire not only of other people, but of other situations. We put off concluding belief for as long as possible.

Asserting, say, a belief that frogs are the highest life form is not intrinsically illogical. Asserting a belief that "life begins at conception" is not illogical. Indeed, as Wittgenstein suggested in the *Tractatus*, it's unclear what it means to call something illogical. If we've postulated things so fundamental they underlie all thought and call these things "logical rules" or "logical laws," then we never contravene these patterns; our mistakes, if such they be, must lie elsewhere. What scientific thought does is to say, I know you want to conclude X and Y, but don't. Not just yet. Not until you've taken all humanly possible steps not to conclude it. Science isn't reason itself, something underlying the world; it's a specific way of proceeding.

My Marine wasn't being irrational: he was reasoning by the same rules as me in saying that his father's situation contradicted what he'd heard about the effects of exposure to the sun. The problem, for me, wasn't the way he was reasoning, but the fact that he stopped his reasoning with what he knew, without throwing open the question to others, who might know other things. He could change his views based on what he experienced personally, but he had not moved to the notion of a public court of appeals that decided such things. For him, belief started on the other side of personal experience. For me, it starts a long way beyond that, if it starts at all.

Power
Scientific types have by and large failed to acknowledge properly the disadvantages of their enterprise, and so make themselves sitting ducks for believers, who correctly point out that belief has advantages that science lacks. Typically scientists are caught within the circular loop of insisting that only science produces objective truth: this is circular because it implies there is no viable alternative to objective truth. And there is. It's belief.

Science needs to argue for the advantages of adopting the scientific viewpoint, and show that they outweigh the disadvantages—not carry on as if it should be clear to all that science is superior to belief. The two are simply two different ways of cutting a cake that cannot, by definition, be further defined: we make a decision to use either a scientific or a belief definition if we go further.

Belief, like personal choice, gives us immense personal power: no one can contradict us. We feel secure. This is precisely the feeling the scientific viewpoint wants to put off for as long as possible, and until after all quarters have been heard from. The scientific point of view is aiming at the establishment of something outside all people by taking into account the data produced by all. Relative security isn't impossible in science, of course, and it's sometimes this that scientific types emphasize. But it comes at the end of a laborious process of public proof and disproof. And even then, as Karl Popper pointed out, you're never 100% sure it won't be disproved at some point.

Many scientists have yelped loudly at this point of Popper's. Perhaps Popper, by saying that scientific theses simply hadn't yet been disproved, appeared to say it was likely they would be: that there was no difference between a thesis that had proved its mettle by being subjected to public scrutiny was no different than one that was newly proposed. The probability narrows to close to zero that a thesis that many people have taken swats at for a long time will one day be shown to have been wrong. But it's never zero. That's Popper's point.

The person who pushes the "I believe" button early on in the discussion and turns away does, admittedly, achieve certainty. Moreover, it's 100% certainty, because that's the goal, the point of pushing this button. It's not true, as scientists usually say, that we need subject ourselves to this laborious and theoretically eternal agon with other people to achieve something like certainty. We can get it without others, far more simply, and have it be more absolute. By saying that only science produces "objective truth," all science does is to state the obvious: what science produces is what science produces. This doesn't decide if others might not rather have something else: say, what belief produces. A believer talking with a scientist is thus always a dialogue of the deaf. My Marine was happy with his "belief"; why should he talk with me?

To make things more complex still, science involves other subjectivities (people) to work in a process that establishes what it calls objective, apersonal, truth. How can many subjectivities produce an objectivity? For the scientist, the fact that something started as somebody's view is irrelevant: it's been shown to be objective truth. For someone who accepts the jump to an objective world, denying that this jump is a jump to a new thing seems ludicrous. It's not that the subjectivity of these reporters' viewpoints count for anything intrinsically, they say. This is just the means to establishing what's true.

But you either accept that this jump is made, or you don't. Someone who insists that "everything is subjective" can't be convinced. It's not necessary to move to this next step; we can be left with the plethora of subjective viewpoints, or explain that one triumphs as a result of other factors entirely. The first is what many humanities and social scientists in recent decades have insisted on. The second is the view, by and large, of those who actually do science. According to those who do science, you solicit the input of other subjectivities in order to establish an objectivity. Accepting the scientific point of view means accepting the connection of these two things, the subjective world of people presenting data, and the objective world that can be deduced by comparing these. For the scientific point of view, what unifies the subjective with the objective is that both reliance on other people and the postulate of an external manifold present alternatives to pushing the "I believe" button, whose presupposition is the self-sufficiency of the individual.

Our own way

Scientific thought tells the individual that his or her way of seeing things is irrelevant. It's understandable that that's not what people want to hear. We want to hear that our own way of seeing things is very important. For an individual, say my Marine, what happened to his own father should be very important. Scientific thought says this may be important at a personal level, but it's irrelevant at a scientific level. From the point of view of science, a father is just an X like any other—a skin, probably, in this example. The fact that he's a father doesn't count.

For this reason the scientific viewpoint is profoundly antithetical to most people. It's not a natural thing. Scientific thinking is a learned skill, and something that has to be practiced continually if it's to be kept alive—assuming we want it to be. It goes against the way we as individuals see the world, and it denies us the ability to be sure about things—given that certainty in science is always a goal put off for as long as possible and hesitantly accepted.

The alternative to this is to see certainty as a postulate, something they can attain as easily as asserting it, as if by reaching out their hands. This is what most people want to do; indeed, as I consider momentarily, it's what all of us do do to a certain extent, no matter whether we're people of faith or people of science: nobody is completely one or the other.

Shrink-wrap

The chief disadvantage of science is that this is not the way most of us conduct most of our lives. Indeed, if we are ever to stride purposefully forward without being afraid of our own shadow, we must simply believe: that the floor won't give way, that our legs will function the way they did yesterday, that we won't cause a bomb to go off by walking, and so on. Even "scientific" people are only so for small portions of their lives; for the rest, to the extent that we manage to be self-sufficient, belief is the filler that takes up fairly quickly after we list the things we know. Belief is the inescapable membrane that shrink-wraps our lives: it's what happens around every moment, all our actions taken as a cumulative whole. We can put off postulating the membrane for a long while in any specific case, while we insist on doing things the scientific way, but for any given individual, an infinitely greater proportion of his or her life is run on the basis of belief. Belief is what's waiting for us when we stop questioning.

Science is a process that's invoked when we question belief. Thus conflicts of science and belief always work in this order: first Belief A, then scientific challenge, then the defensiveness of belief reasserting itself, that we can call Belief A'. Belief A would therefore be something like: the world was created 6,000 years ago with just the animals it now has. The scientific challenge is: it seems much older and there are traces of many animals that no longer exist. Belief A' would therefore be: it is *too* 6,000 years old and has always been the way it is.

This is the case where belief is foregrounded enough to take center stage. Belief A', the self-conscious version of Belief A, is always at a disadvantage. But the fact is, all of life is permeated with versions of Belief A that are never challenged: even those who adopt the scientific explanation in this particular case can never do without things of the type of Belief A.

Hume's genius was to see that things of the sort of Belief A are always waiting in the wings to take over at the end of all scientific explanation. But this doesn't mean that they're things of the sort of Belief A'. They don't substitute for science, they retreat until science is finished. When we focus on the conflict between belief and science, it's always by definition things of the sort of Belief A' we're talking about. It's science that turns Belief A into Belief A' by challenging it.

Other people

Other people's views matter to a scientific viewpoint; they don't, by contrast, matter to one that insists on the primacy of belief. You can push the "I believe" button immediately, but if you do so, you limit severely the number of people you'll have in your corner. If that doesn't matter to you, there's no reason not to do it.

Most of us, at some point, think other people matter. At this point we accept the scientific viewpoint. Religion is right to say that science is secular: it makes us think of the here and now. Someone who insists on living in his or her own world of belief can, in theory, never be pulled from that world. Science tries by providing a forum for the points of view of other people. It's an edgy, uncertain world. Much better in some ways merely to say what is and stick to it.

Yet the disadvantages of belief are also clear: those who privilege belief are always liable to being, as we say in the military, blind-sided. Their worlds can be more utterly destroyed than the world of someone who asks for continuous outside information and deals with it as it comes across the transom. The lure of belief is real, and it's strong. At some point nearly all of us probably give in to it: and why not? It's part of our nature too.

Predicting others

Typically, the same people who reserve the right to complete self-determination in the form of "belief" and "choice" want to be able to say that they know exactly how others will act. There's probably a human tendency to make the assumption that We can change and They can't. As Sartre would point out, we as the perceiver always seem boundaryless and amenable to change to ourselves; we are always in the process of Becoming. Others, by contrast, are solid, or appear to be so. After all, we see them from the outside, their shells—that seem so solid. And Wittgenstein draws a balloon-like shape in the *Tractatus* and observes acerbically: Our visual field is not like this. He then notes that if he wrote a book called *The World as I Found It*, it would begin with a description of feet, legs, belly, and arms. To describe the face we'd have to have recourse to a mirror. (The writer Bruce Duffy published a novel called just this, a fictionalized version of the life of the philosopher.) Wittgenstein's point is that we seem to ourselves intrinsically constituent of the world in a way that others aren't.

Frequently this takes the form of saying that we can predict the actions of others by learning about what they believe, their religion. Following the 2001 attack on the World Trade Center, this assertion was frequently heard regarding Muslims. Islam is X and Y (most frequent assertion: violent). How do we know? We read their scriptures, and they believe in their scriptures. QED.

The problem is, justification of action only works in one direction: from the action to the justification. We can't go back to an assertion in scripture and conclude how people who believe in it, or purport to believe in it, will be acting. But the attempt shows that belief and analysis are yin and yang, things we engage in alternately or depending on our point of view: the aesthetic sense of life involves reveling in the relationship between them, following as one mutates into the other.

The aesthetic sense, however, doesn't insist that belief give way to analysis—a common misconception, confusing expecting a shift to insisting that the shift take place here and now. The aesthetic sense isn't impatient with people who are riding a wave of belief, only aware that at some point it will crash, and the person be dumped out on the sand.

Rudolph the Red-Nosed Reindeer

Because texts are static in time and finite, we can't say what they'll lead to in the future. No Martian, appealing to the holy scripture of a scriptural religion, could ever arrive at an accurate picture of what people calling themselves adherents of this religion actually do. What reader in 1830 of the Book of Mormon could have postulated the Mormon Tabernacle Choir? What reader of the Gospel of Mark (or indeed the entire Christian and Jewish Bibles) could have postulated America's Christmastime orgy of consumption? Later permutations such as Frosty the Snowman or Rudolph the Red-Nosed Reindeer? What outsider who didn't know how the Koran is in fact used as the basis for people's lives would be able to generate the life of the family of a Pakistani immigrant doctor in New York or suburban Washington, D.C.?

How, our Martin would wonder more generally, did a desert religion such as Christianity end up with the trappings of snow and cold it has acquired? Even in Florida and Los Angeles Christmas is celebrated with fir trees rather than palm trees and with white spray "snow" on shop windows. We can of course explain the origin of these things once we have them: evergreen trees standing for eternal life, Martin Luther bringing one inside (for the same reason holly and mistletoe become associated with Christianity), Queen Victoria bringing one to England through her German husband Albert, and its transplantation to the New World. But we can't postulate this particular sequence of events from the perspective of the text itself.

Seeing how a revealed scripture is in fact applied in everyday life is like running a recording of a game of "Telephone," where one person in the circle at the parlor game whispers the starting phrase in the ear of the next person and so on around. The point of the game is always to laugh at the divergence between the end result and the original phrase. There's nothing in the Christian Bible that prepares us for Rudolph the Red-Nosed Reindeer. Given Rudolph, however, we can trace the thread backwards and see how we got where we are: If you have the thread of Ariadne in the maze you can get back to where you started.

It's in the Koran

Typically the proof, such as it is, that Islam is intrinsically violent and so must be countered with violence, is that the Koran contains references to "jihad," variously translated as "striving" or "holy war." See?

The argument goes? It says right here (Sura 47), "When ye encounter the infidels, strike off their heads." The attempt is being made to intuit the string forward, to say what this must in fact lead to down the line: this is always misguided; instead, we have to look at what is, from which we can provide the explanation of how we got here.

To be sure, those out to get certainty from the Koran usually concede, verses like this find their counter in verses like that from Sura 2, "Let there be no compulsion in religion." They stick to their position that we can *too* give a bottom line to a complex text by pointing out that revelations seem to change over time, and usually it's the later ones that are held to "abrogate" the former. Earlier revelations seem merely to discourage alcohol; later ones forbid it. Earlier revelations seem quite conciliatory toward the Jews (the original direction for prayer was toward Jerusalem, changed to Mecca). Later revelations are harder-toned.

Yet how much can we as outsiders reading the Koran draw from chronology? How much can insiders? When it matters, it apparently matters—Islam as a whole seems to have decided for the prohibition of alcohol (but permission of other narcotics). But most of the time it doesn't. All of the Koran is the word of God, to be evoked when it seems appropriate. There's no sense that the words of God are arranged on a scale which includes at any point "don't have to pay attention to these because early revelations."

To make things more complex, chronology is something we have to conclude with the Koran, or assert. It's not something anyone is sure about. Sometimes, indeed, the conclusion of chronology is completely circular, based on what we think the position taken by the text would have been when. Generally speaking, the shorter Suras toward the back of the Koran (Suras are arranged from longest to shortest) tend to be the earlier. But the correlation between long and late isn't absolute; sometimes a Sura is long because it's made up of bits and pieces whose dating is unclear. Thus it's possible to have an earlier verse in a later Sura, or the reverse, and frequently the conclusion that it is earlier is based precisely on what attitude it takes toward the subject at hand. If our position is that later verses always override earlier ones, and we decide what the later ones are based on what they say, we've decided what the bottom line to the word of God is and are going backwards from there. In the case of the "no compulsion in religion," this is part of a Sura that should by rights be later than the shorter 47.

More fundamentally, though Muslims may be aware of these alterations, the Koran is neither arranged nor taught chronologically; it's a whole, and all of it is the word of God. (This is a fact about Islam we have to ask about; we can't know without asking how the Koran is taught.) Rationalist outsiders want to insist that chronology is determinative, which it doesn't seem to be to Muslims on most issues, any more than chronology of transmission is a big issue for Christians. Scholars tell us the Gospel of Mark came first, but what Believer needs know this or cares? There are many divergences between the versions of the three closest synoptic Gospels (Matthew, Mark, and Luke), and even more with respect to John. But it doesn't seem to bother anyone.

For believers, views can simultaneously be "corrected" and still have all versions be God's unalterable will. If they are, they are; figure it out if you like and can, or look for someone to do it for you. But nothing is riding on your figuring it out: that may well be one of those things you die not understanding, at which point all will be made clear. The category of things we die not having answers to is a huge one, after all.

Satanic Verses

The issue of correction was behind the international uproar regarding Salman Rushdie's 1988 novel *The Satanic Verses*, which used as one of its bases the well-documented case referred to in the Koran itself (17:73-75; 22:52-53) in Sura 53:17-22 where, as tradition has it, Satan interjected words that the Prophet later removed. The words in question say that the daughters of the moon god, who had names and were independently worshipped, were in fact worthy of worship—an apparent departure from the insistence of other revelation at the time insisting that God is One. In the definitive edition of the revelation, the words do not therefore appear in the text. Only the traces of the removal remain (above) and the tradition that they were once there.

This, of course, is a different sort of re-thinking than that apparently represented by altering positions on various issues. In this case a reason is given for the emendation: Satan had intervened, and was countered. Theologically speaking, there is no cause for alarm at this on the part of believing Muslims. It's not logically necessary to conclude, as some commentators (including Rushdie) apparently do, that this suggests there are other passages of the Koran which are similarly corrupted but have not been corrected. Only someone who fails to assume that all actually in (as opposed to: not in) the Koran is the word of God would conclude this.

Most Muslims would reject the imputation that the religion was theirs to mold, say by waking up one morning and deciding to do things differently; most would claim that they were following the unalterable world of God. Few religions of the Book, as the Koran calls religions such as Judaism and Christianity with revealed scriptures, accept what seems to outsiders the case: that their religions change. Most always they insist on the opposite, as a link to the revelation behind them.

Even those who accept that changes are possible rarely have the sense that they can personally influence a turn-around. Changes are instead incremental and in most cases beyond the scope or volition of individuals. So adherents of a religion with a revealed scripture usually find it impossible to influence it individually, or refuse to try for doctrinal reasons, and aren't conscious of doing so as a group. Changing a religion is instead like turning a battleship, or the way one drifts to a new course without people really knowing it's doing so: it only happens slowly and in a lumbering fashion.

Role of the text

Reading a text, whether sacred or secular, doesn't answer the question, What role does the text actually play in people's lives? This doesn't mean: What do they say if asked? That might well be only lip service. More to the point might be: How much contact do they actually have with it? What is the nature of that contact? What do they do with that contact? For many self-proclaimed Christians of a certain generation, having the Bible prominently displayed in the living room was enough.

The Koran is in classical Arabic, recited both as an art form and to formalize agreements. Many of the people who hear it learn what to do by being schooled in fiqh, the practices of daily life (ablutions, prayers, marriage and divorce rules, and so on). It's roughly comparable to the way Jews learn a bit of the Hebrew Torah for their bar or bat mitzvah, recite it syllabically, and then comment on it as part of the ceremony. There's always a rabbi to keep you more or less in the normal bounds of what most people have said about this passage. Is a memorized text an understood text?

For adherents of a religion with a holy text, the text isn't a map spread out on a table, where we can easily compare divergent passages. It's instead the real country that surrounds us. We can go wherever we want within it; the country doesn't care where we are, but at any given time we're only in one place. That means we cherry-pick texts, like wandering through an orchard of trees in fruit, grabbing a handful here and a handful there, going back to a particularly succulent tree if we have the yen. Within the holy text, as within the orchard, there is no compulsion. One tree is as good as another.

The history of how the cherry-picking has gone is the establishment of organized religion. These function as the changing right-here right-now interface of practical application. For centuries, Roman Catholicism, the only Christianity available, rejected individual reading of the Bible by the faithful. Protestantism changed all that. Now, under the influence of Protestantism, Catholicism does so as well. But it still controls that transmission to a degree, dipping into both books of the Bible for any passage ranging from Jewish history and law to the erotic poetry of the Psalms to the apocalyptic vision of St. John, read aloud as part of the Mass and finished off with the ritual phrase: "The Word of God."

It's the goal of all words, not just the Word of God, to control all things past themselves. But the fact is that they exist in time: they may be eternal, but we are not, and we decide how to apply them, if at all. That's where the necessity to cherry-pick comes in. At any given point in time we can only be doing one thing. How do we decide which thing? If we're smiting the infidel can also be doing other things? Is it acceptable to smite the infidel first and then do the other things? Under what circumstances does which take precedence? How do we know what to do at any given point in time among the thousands of things we're told to do? This the text itself, by definition, can't tell us: the text is only the orchard. How to harvest or try the fruit is the business of the organized religion. Thus the knowledge to be gained by "going back to the source" of the revealed book is limited.

Stripping away layers

What we actually do with religions is like taking a path off a path off a path off a path. And this means, we fail to follow up many paths that might have been. They either dry up and fall off the tree diagram, or lie fallow until someone goes back and tries them. And that means that we can't find what people really do or spend their time on (say, "Rudolph the Red-Nosed Reindeer" played ad infinitum in a million suburban malls from October to January) in the earliest layers, the revelation itself: all that's happened since then has itself become part of the temporal string.

Reformers periodically try and strip off a certain number of recent levels of development: Wahabi Islam is one example of this, so too is the Protestant reformation, so too is the Church of Christ in the U.S., so is Methodism, so is Quakerism, so is the Church of Jesus Christ of Latter Day Saints. Their claim is that however many levels they want to strip off have nothing to do with the real religion, to which they are returning.

Some do this by returning to the same text, some deliver new texts (Church of Christ of Latter Day Saints is like Islam in holding that the new text, in the case of LDS *The Book of Mormon*, supersedes the old.) What's amusing to an outsider is reformers who try to strip away a small number of layers: religious protesters in the U.S. who want the Christmas carols of the nineteenth century rather than those of the twentieth, for example. It's "putting Christ in Christmas" to sing about the snow that lay around when Jesus Christ our Lord was born, following a Victorian invention rather than an American derivation.

Zeno's paradoxes

Someone trying to figure out a religion, which is a living breathing whole, from the outside—say from its revealed writings—is like Dr. Frankenstein trying to make a living being out of the fragments. You need the spark of life; the text is merely the parts. When we read a revealed text to learn about a religion, it's as if we were building up the religion piece by piece: without the belief that makes it whole, it's bound to look like fragments. Our point of view that of an arrow speeding toward a target it has yet to reach. According to one of Zeno's paradoxes, the arrow should not by rights ever reach the target: It diminishes first by half the distance to the target, then half of the remaining distance, than half of the distance that remains then, and so on, infinitely sub-dividing the distance but never actually reaching where it's going.

For believers the arrow is already at the target: they don't have to prove that it gets there. The process of an outsider laboriously piecing together text to see if it justifies a religion is like proving the arrow never reaches the target. But if it does, it does, and saying it shouldn't—as many outsider readers of holy texts, full of their contradictions and "mistakes" tend to do—is merely silly.

How to sell your daughter into slavery

For a living faith, contradictions don't count, and you don't have to justify what you're focusing on: all of it is fair game. Most Christians simultaneously claim the arcane rules in the Torah are the "word of God," and would never think of following them. These include as rules for selling our daughters into slavery, Exodus 21:7; rules against men cutting their hair, Lev 19.27; rules against planting two crops in the same field, Lev. 19:19; or rules against having contact with women during their menstrual period, Lev 15:19-24. Yet apparently we can cherry-pick individual rules from such lineups to follow, chronology disregarded. People who cut their hair and wear clothes made of two kinds of thread (Lev 19:19) sometimes do insist that homosexuality is an "abomination" (Lev 18:22)—as for that matter is eating shellfish (Lev. 11:10), something they may be willing or eager to do. We can't use the text to justify why we'd be interested in homosexuality being an "abomination" (scholars suggest that this is a misleading translation, that in fact should be something more like: source of ritual impurity) and (assuming we're not

Orthodox Jews) shellfish not. And even Orthodox Jews don't sell their daughters into slavery: they've cherry-picked too.

Nor, by definition, can a holy text tell us how great a role individual bits will play in our life. Sects of Christianity that play with poisonous snakes as part of their worship make much of a single phrase from Mark 17-18 (Jesus is speaking): "In My name shall they cast out devils; they shall speak with new tongues; They shall take up serpents; and if they drink any deadly thing, it shall not hurt them." Others object that this isn't Christian; after all "the Bible: (Jesus is again speaking) also tells us: "Thou shalt not tempt the Lord thy God" (Luke 14:12). Each of these two positions will claim it's Christian and the justification for choosing one over the other can't come from the text itself. Who says snake-handling can't be the center of things?

Literal vs. metaphoric

There's a vast spectrum of application ranging from general to specific: the text itself can't tell us where the interpretation is going to fall; only people actually taking the paths can do that. One interpretation is to deny precisely this: Christian fundamentalists do so, asserting that they have gotten back to the original text and have dispensed with all the intermediate steps. In order to hold this, they typically hold that only two readings of scripture are possible, the literal and the metaphoric: they follow the literal. Such as, for example, the question of whether the six days in which the world was created were "real" or "metaphoric" days.

But at most they can only resolve one such question in favor of the literal; the whole Bible can't be merely literal. If it is, it can't stand as the basis for a religion. We have to decide how literally to take the stories about Jesus. If they are only what they say, then their application is limited to describing, as best hearsay and repeated stories can, the doings of a historical person two thousand years ago. The presupposition of the religion has to be that they mean more than they say. The parables of Jesus are another good example: the same people who insist that "day" be read literally typically insist that "lost sheep" doesn't mean lost sheep, and that the actions of various characters are meant to be generalized. The Good Samaritan's actions should serve as a model for us: we should be "good Samaritans" too.

In fact, there's no such thing as having a religion based on "literal" readings of revealed texts. When we're told about one tribe fighting its neighbor, this can't be merely history, there has to be some lesson for us in it. Religion answers questions like this: How can we get a guide for action out of something that was a specific geometrical point on the time line that has continued to recede from us as the years have gone by? Are we meant to emulate the Prophet? Jesus? Or merely heed what they say? Both Christianity and Islam have decided for emulation, but the very fabric of the religion is determined by how we emulate. Islamic tradition, for example, has it that the Prophet was naturally circumcised (lacked a foreskin). For this reason Muslim boys are circumcised at puberty. Could we determine what color the Prophet's hair was and dye all people's hair? Have everyone wear a cloak such as he wore? (Both hairs and cloak are preserved as relics in Istanbul's Topkapi Palace.) Why choose one quality for literal emulation and let others go?

Time elapsing between the production of revelation and the present day has answered many such questions by taking specific paths; these are part of the belief system, not extraneous to it. Most organized religions are sufficiently self-aware that they insist that this is so, and add that the paths taken were inevitable, because correct. This requires the additional codicil of saying, as the Prophet said, "My community will never agree on error." And the Catholic Church claims its Pope is infallible when speaking *ex cathedra*, and traces its genesis (and the source of the Pope's authority) back to St. Peter. This builds change into the process, and makes conclusions drawn from going back to the original sources only partially satisfactory, something that has to be justified on the grounds of later corruption of practice.

How Islamic is he?

But let's say that we can in fact do what I say we can't: say once and for all that, for example, the Koran clearly is trying to compel us to do X under circumstances Y. We still don't know how "Islamic" (if defined as doing X under circumstances Y) an individual or group of individuals is going to be. If all did something we're not expecting we might conclude they're not Islamic, even if they said they were. Hey! we'd say, running after them. That's not fair! My book here says you're supposed to be doing X, Y and Z, not A, B, and C! How impressed do you think they'd be? Not that having people act differently than you say they have to act is a disproof of such a contention. If you define a religion in a certain way and so conclude that people are bound to act in accordance with that way they can still diverge from this, at least on the surface, because they're (a) biding their time or (b) momentarily in re-group mode or (c) slackers. Or perhaps, merely doing other things.

No: from reading a holy text, we can't conclude what the actual fabric of life will be like, how often specific things will be evoked (unless part of the content deals with frequency, as for example in the case of prayer for Islam, Ramadan fasting, or the Hadj) and what else will be there. Saying that someone is a Muslim (or having him or her say it) doesn't mean that if we are a fly on the wall with a Muslim for a day that we'll see only things reading the Koran (even assuming we have a standard way of reading it and understanding it) have led us to expect. It may prepare us for more things than reading another religion's holy book will prepare us for, but it won't prepare us for everything

If we observe a Muslim going about the business of living in the old city of Algiers, or in Fez, we may well think this person really and truly Muslim, part of the image of heat, dust, and camels, with the wailing of the muezzin that we associate with the Muslim life. But what if this person lives next door to us in another suburban McMansion and makes snowmen when we do? How much of this is a Muslim life? How much was the life in Fez, and how much was merely a local variant? How close are our lives in the USA to early Christian camel drivers almost two thousand years ago? We may emphasize what for us seems the absolute identity (we too are baptized), but a Martian would see many more divergences than similarities: we focus on what we choose to focus on.

This divergence of view is behind the perception we call the exotic: an outsider notices what's different. An exotic view of a religion is unlikely to jibe with its reality for those who live it. The views of many Westerners trying to make sense of Islam based on reading the Koran are such exotic views: look! A camel! For the person who owns it, that's just like the family car. It's not that the exotic point of view is illegitimate—which is the conclusion of a lot of "post-colonial" studies (if you don't see things our way, you're wrong). It's just that we can't say from this outsider's point of view what the people on the inside are actually up to.

Many things simply escape the purview of religions. No limited body of revelation or words can be so broad as to regulate all aspects of life. We only notice the actions that the religion seems to have an opinion about, not the ones that aren't touched. To be sure, the things a religion has, or seems to have, an opinion about, are what characterize the religion. Islam, unlike Christianity, may tell you how to go to the bathroom (use left hand, say the following prayer). But neither religion controls everything.

Even so, we will be surprised by what surprises us only because we, unlike the people to whom it is old hat, don't take it for granted. We're bound to notice the administrative duties demanded by the religion because we don't do them. Say, that our Muslim host excuses himself and arranges himself on the floor to pray at the appointed time, for example—if we weren't expecting this. Or the way our strict Brahmin acquaintance avoids eating the food we, as non-Brahmins, have prepared. Or the way a Christian may wear around his or her neck a small version of a Roman instrument of criminal torture that s/he touches in moments of stress. To those who live with these things, they are quotidian, and hence far less defining of life in the minds of the people who live with them than they are for us.

It's true that for someone coming from the secular West, where we can get through the whole day without mentioning God except to swear, suddenly encountering the ceaseless "God willing" or "God be praised" that is part of phrasing in an Islamic world will strike us. Perhaps part of the negative reaction is jealousy on the part of Christian fundamentalists, who would like "Seasons Greetings" forcibly changed to "Merry Christmas" whenever it appears?

Similarly, a Martian might well remark the amount of time we spend taking care of our bodies, from the tooth-brushing to makeup to gym time, to food preparation, to eating, to excreting. If their system requires none of this (say, their bodies take care of themselves until one day they simply fall apart, being given enough energy for one lifetime at birth and never having to spend any of that life on getting more), it will seem to them that this is all we do with our lives. To us, who take these for granted, this isn't so.

Here and there

Once here, you can explain the connection to there. But you can't derive here from there. Nor can we prove how things will develop in the future. All you can do is find out what people actually do, how they actually react to outsiders who express opinions, and enter the fray. That is, see things with the aesthetic sense of life.

But that's true of all human interactions. A well known source of male frustration is the fact that men can't "prove" that women do X and Y, nor can we conclude from saying that a person is a woman that she'll do A or B. A lot of time could be saved if men, instead of discussing women among themselves—or women men for that matter—simply looked at what in fact is the case, right here, right now. From this they might begin to draw some distinctions between things more typical and less typical, more local and less local. But all this is the result of observation. None of it can be concluded *a priori*.

Human beings aren't scientific; only science is scientific. Yet at the same time science isn't something removed from the scale of things people do; it's a human undertaking that tries to transcend the particular. The same is true of religion. The two clash, but provide alternative explanations and fulfill alternative needs. The aesthetic sense of life undertsands that there will be people fixed in one of these more than the other, at least for certain times: it makes no effort to predict where people will be at any given time (waiting, say, for belief to give way for science, or insisting that it do so), only notes when the change takes place.

Science is something people do. So is religion. Which is why we need the aesthetic sense of life. We can look at these things, consider how we react to them, interact with them, without ever thinking we're going to get one to dismantle the other.

Chapter Seven
Modernity and the Aesthetic Sense

THE AESTHETIC SENSE ALLOWS US to consider the givens of our time in a way that questions them, notes them, compares them to things they aren't, and appreciates their good qualities, but doesn't end up by saying that, because they are the modern, they are perfect. Nor need the aesthetic sense go to the opposite extreme and conclude that because a time is gone and so no longer painful to live through, it must have been ideal. All presents are contingent, our own included: what makes our own present different from other presents is simply the fact that it's our own. We can't travel to the past the way we can travel to a different place, sense the world outside, but we can at least imagine that world and see how it differs from our own.

Topkapi

Another way to see the modern is as whatever we take for granted. Thus we sense modernity most strongly in seeing what it isn't. A visit to the Topkapi Palace in Istanbul, which served as the palace of the Ottoman sultans until the mid-nineteenth century, when they moved up the Bosporus to a frenetically ornate French-style palace called Dolmabahçe, may cause us to sense the nature of our world in comparison to others. Topkapi Palace isn't a palace in the Western sense, more a collection of smaller individual pavilions, some mazes of rooms (the treasury), some single rooms set entirely with the blue and red tiles we associate with the Ottoman Empire, in some cases a library or receiving room. They're clustered around green swards, arranged in order of importance of outer and inner, according to their proximity to the places central to the exercise of the Sultan's authority.

One of these buildings is laid off to the side, larger and internally complex: the harem. This is a warren of sleeping cells, group rooms, courtyards, and baths. Tourists on the guided (and only possible) tour of the Harem are encouraged to take photos of a "black eunuch," as the guide calls it, posed in diorama display behind glass off one of the outrageously tiled hallways. There visitors see a department store mannequin of what seems a young, well-muscled male (one of his arms is bare), wearing a turban and a caftan-style robe, standing as if to offer service to a more elaborately-dressed woman. The color of the plastic of the male doll is, as advertised, black: jet black. The woman is pink. The robe covers any evidence of the mannequin's possessing, or lacking, private parts. For that matter, most mannequins lack private parts and so are in this sense eunuchs. So the viewer wonders what makes this mannequin more of a eunuch than others endowed only with a slight bulge, rather than any package approaching anatomic correctness. But of course it's the man represented by this plastic jet-black doll who's supposed to be a eunuch, not the doll. The guide explains that the only intact male allowed in this part of the palace—post-pubescent, presumably, as the children lived here too, of both sexes—was the sultan. Take your pictures now, please.

A few minutes later the guide explains that the concubines, whose sleeping cubicles off a courtyard (separated only by curtains) we are looking at, were highly educated gifts to the sultan from other peoples, had to learn a musical instrument, and retired at 30. "What happened to them then?" a tourist asks. "They returned to their home countries," says the guide—as if they had been cultural visitors back to spread the word of the greatness of the capital city.

All the emphasis in this tour for Westerners is on the talents of the concubines, the fact that they were given an education. The fact that they were sex slaves is never mentioned, and the fact that they were slaves of any sort acknowledged only in passing. As the guide says matter-of-factly, "Slavery was part of the Ottoman Empire." After all, modern-day Turkey has moved beyond that. And of course, slavery was part of the West as well, outlawed in British dominions a mere three decades before disappearing from America.

Strangely enough, this world does not seem unmodern, merely different: it's too different from our own world for something to spring into relief as an alternative. The aesthetic sense requires a combination of same and different in the world outside to achieve the patterning that is its basis; similarly it requires a combination of things we take for granted and things we don't for us to see the pattern in a time-travel world. I find it not in the older Ottoman palace, but in the newer.

Marble Palace

Another guide, in the furiously overwrought but completely Dolmabahçe Palace—whose twin is the rotting Marble Palace down a pullulating side street in Calcutta, its dank over-filled rooms decorated with oil paintings whose colors are long mouldered, sliding down the canvas from sheer humidity—is more Americanized, more fluent, and more voluble. Before entering the Harem, which he tells us, rather unconvincingly, means only "family quarters," he discourses at great length on the Western image of the Harem as the place where the Sultans went to fulfil their wildest sexual fantasies. In fact, he assures visitors, it wasn't that at all. Given how dull they are, it's easy to believe this.

The rooms for the concubines here, in this Western palace exemplary in its public spaces of the conviction that more of everything—crystal, gilt, silver and gold—is more, are striking in their very plainness, their aura of being prison cells masquerading as rooms. The real cells, barely large enough for bedding, product of an earlier time in the Topkapi Palace, seem closer to the rabbit warren we imagine and so are less striking. These are plain rooms, by our standards, with enormously high ceilings, as if adding space in an unusable direction, furnished with Western furniture of a not very prepossessing design. Indeed, we don't know if the furniture is anything like the original: the guide explains that these rooms were emptied when the Sultan was deposed in 1922 by Atatürk and that we have no written records of what it was like to live in the Harem. Still, it seems probable the original furniture was as forlorn as this: the rooms themselves are plain, just down the hall from the unbelievably ornate audience chamber—the one that holds the largest chandelier (of English crystal) in Europe. The rooms of the queen mother, the "Valide Sultan," look out onto the Bosporus and the Asian shore a boat ride away.

The suites of the four legitimate wives are hardly more appealing than those of the concubines. They are slightly larger the single rooms of the concubines, but are still prisons, and not very ornate ones, like the maze of tubes that a hamster can run in before ending up where it started. Each wife, the guide tells us, lived with her own children in her own tiny cluster of these palace rooms whose high ceilings must have been a daily reminder of the opulence she actually glimpsed only in the presence of the Sultan (the most luxurious room in the Harem was the reception room for the Sultan, used only on his visits); the public rooms. including the one with the huge chandelier, were something the women could only view from behind a semi-circular grill from a hidden hallway in the next story up, near the ceiling of the audience room: a hallway sealed with iron doors at both ends led to the confined quarters was a place they could only go into on ceremonial occasions, and then only to peek out from behind the grills down at the men carrying out their business below.

The Western visitor is repulsed. We have a visceral reaction nowadays against castrating men to use them as guardians of women, of physical sequestering of women. And yet in this world, it was completely normal. What throws this into relief is the very normalcy of these rooms, their plainness, the fact that they seem so of our world. Yet what went on here: this, we sense, is not us: it is not "modern."

Repellent
The reason all these things seem so repellent to a Westerner, I think, is our presupposition that an entire human life should not be put to the service of another's in quite this absolute a way. You can't deny one person his manhood (as we'd probably say) or another her liberty so that someone else can live the life or she wants to live. Each person has to line up at the starting line and get a chance, with no artificial constraints. If the people contravening this wear different clothes and live in different places, we tend merely to shrug and move on. But if they live in mdern palaces and do un-modern things, we tend to find the contrast upsetting.

Modernity, it seems, involves tthe assumption that you can't make structures using the very being of people as the bricks and mortar; pre-modernity assumed you could—a pre-modernity that lasted until 1922 in the Ottoman Empire. It's a relatively recent point of view, articulated for the Enlightenment by Kant. We're supposed to treat people as ends in themselves. Not that the Ottoman Empire was the only one in the world that held such presuppositions. In the Museum of the Ancient Orient in Istanbul, palace friezes from Assyria (others are in New York and Paris) show court eunuchs, as tall as the bearded kings and winged gods but with fat faces, and unmarred by hair. America legally kept slaves until the end of the Civil War. Mauritania only legally abolished slavery in the 1970s, and according to reports still continues it de facto. Increasingly we rebel against the notion that women should be kept in a cage until their male feels like taking them out.

Natural vs. artificial
As part of its point of view, modernity acknowledges that there's a difference between natural impediments, which we can do nothing about, and artificial ones. Physical beauty might be something we can't help, as is ugliness: we don't say that everyone should be born pretty. But we might well take steps to make sure that ugly people get the same chances. Similarly, we might acknowledge that some people will be born into loving and supportive households that help them grow up strong and independent, and others won't. But we might do things to try and "level the playing field" for the people who don't get this leg up.

The distinction between natural and artificial advantages or disadvantages can also be viewed with the aesthetic sense of life—accepting that the distinction exists, but questioning each case where we think we've found an example of it. For the trouble with the metaphor of "leveling the playing field" is that we have to decide what constitutes the field and what constitutes individual variations—and this dividing line is perennially open to re-negotiation and debate. Players on a field have what we call "natural talent," related to physical prowess, parents who encouraged them, a place to hone their skills, and perhaps natural intelligence. Are all of these qualities merely individual variations that they should be allowed to use to win? Or are they structural variations that should be leveled with the field?

One way to make sure we've completely "leveled the field" is to proclaim all qualities field qualities, and none individual ones. That way we merely decide that every game is going to be a tie. That's the direction we've gone in with what's called "political correctness" and "affirmative action." We just announce how we want things to come out (say, a certain percentage of university slots to be won by people of color), and make it happen. There, we say: the playing field is level.

This sees all benefits as structural rather than personal, and denies the legitimacy of any of them. The equally extreme alternative is what this is a rebellion against: seeing all advantages as personal, things that just happened to be. But this of course presupposes a world run by and for those with the advantages. Like the Sultans, and their European counterparts before the French Revolution with their "divine right of kings," those getting the benefits of something will never see their benefit as something unnatural. To them it seems perfectly natural. Men think it natural for them to have advantages women don't get. Straight people think it natural to have advantages gay people don't get. And so on. So there's no agreement on what constitutes the kind of impediment, in the West, that should be flattened. Let's say the West pays reparations to the descendents of slaves. Why should they not get reparations from the countries that sold them to the Westerners to begin with? One very good reason is that these are not the countries that can pay: you only ask for money from people who have money.

Even "political correctness" isn't applied with respect to all advantages or disadvantages, only to this year's hot topics: nowadays we use up all our energy arguing over things like skin color and sexuality. Yet we take the help or hindrance of other qualities for granted as natural, in just the same way the pre-Revolutionary aristocracy took for granted their divine right. The accident of someone being born into a First-World country is one of those unjustifiable facts that determines that person's life: rare are the people who argue that this is an illegitimate structural leg-up. This fact transcends even the ability of legislation to right things—say, the equivalent of the American civil rights laws for the citizens of all countries. Even the most liberal campaigners in America tend to limit the change they're agitating for to within its borders: they want (say) brown-skinned people in this country to be treated in a certain way, not alter the plight of brown-skinned people elsewhere, who almost invariably are in a much worse situation than those within the United States.

So it's not true that modernity is the complete freeing of the individual: all it does is proclaim certain advantages structural, not all. In the West we didn't castrate people so they wouldn't threaten our women; we did so in order for them to sing as sopranos past puberty—and also because castrati sound subtly different than boy sopranos. This was deemed justifiable: it was, after all, in the service of God. Or was it the service of the Popes who listened to them sing, in the Sistine Chapel among other places? But we don't do that any more. The last castrato died before World War I; his name was Alessandro Moreschi—recordings of his failing but strangely evanescent voice exist.

Anyone suggesting that the Catholic Church's vow of celibacy for clergy, apparently roundly ignored by many priests, constitutes a way of denying personhood on the level of castration would have to be prepared for a fight: to us this seems different, because we accept celibacy the way we don't accept castration. And indeed, there are many structures of the modern world that end up using the individual as part of a larger structure, theoretically indistinguishable from the way slaves spent their lives toiling for others in the pre-modern world and its holdouts, such as the American south, or the palace of the Ottoman sultans until 1922.

It can be argued too that nothing better gives the lie to the West's self-image as offering every person self-worth than the fact that we still engage in war, the ultimate denial of selfhood to the individual. War uses people as cogs in a machine. To be sure, your whole life isn't even ground out in a cotton field, or washing clothes for others. But it is scooped up with the lives of hundreds, perhaps thousands, of others that are all thrown at one objective, which they may or may not achieve. Or they're mowed down as the result of someone else's trying to achieve an objective measured in thousands of lives.

The aesthetic sense of life can help us understand modernity without having us feel superior in that we get to be modern.

Obituaries
Not that this alters the fact that there is something horrible to us about the wives' chambers in Dolmabahçe Palace, even more horrible than the even smaller chambers of the concubines—who after all were slaves—in Topkapi Palace. Their servitude seems worse for having been

lived out in the midst of such opulence, with the knowledge that the only view you would ever have out your window, if you were lucky enough to have a window, was that of the never-changing Bosporus and the Asian shore, that you would spend decades until you died in these four rooms—and then to have your world cleaned out in a revolution, and have guides say that we have no record of how life here was lived.

But how different is this from lives of which we have a record? I am always struck by obituaries. One would think that a life had not been lived in vain that ended with a large obituary in *The New York Times,* perhaps beginning with "Pulitzer Prize-winning poet X Dies" (on the day I write this, it was Stanley Kunitz). Yet the point of obituary is always to tell a story: what doesn't fit isn't part of the story. The character is sketched, the career highlights are alluded to—career always defined in very narrow terms, the way we answer a cocktail party question, "What do you do?" Perhaps some human interest (he loved gardening) or even a gaffe or two, if not too serious, is included to make better reading. One obituary that caught my eye was for an almost 90-year-old man; the headline was that in his 70s he laid claim to an island in the Potomac River that later was declared not to be his: this was his brush with celebrity, so the rest of his career fell into line behind this. Was this really the meaning of his life? Such obituaries cure us of the belief that a journalist's "take" on our life can in any way redeem our life, or give it meaning. Obituaries are articles in newspapers whose content is determined by the fact that they need a journalistic "hook": they're not there to somehow do justice to the person, but to fit him or her into the same narrative as other events in the paper.

This may be clearest at the next level down of celebrity: not the Pulitzer-Prize-winning poet but someone whose obituary is entitled "Secretary to X" where X is a name we recognize. Few people can see this as conferring value on the dead person's life; at best it gives us a reason for reading the article. What about someone like Rosa Parks, forever frozen as the young woman sitting on the bus? That was a genuinely admirable act, but Rosa Parks couldn't have said it would have the effect it did. To write her whole life as a postscript to that one moment hardly does justice to the women, we think: it's as unfair as using a person in the way we think unmodern.

We live our whole life, it seems, and if we're lucky become a tag line, the one thing that makes good reading. Who can confuse this with having lived a purposeful life? And how many people go out without such a printed memorial at all? Have they any less failed to be? The presupposition that's foisted upon us as children is that people who win the Pulitzer Prize thereby enter a sort of Valhalla. But what if no one remembers who they are? At most we read the article and think how fleeting fame is, that we don't even recognize the names any more. What if we remember the name but don't read their works? Does this fact give value to the lives of the deceased? What if we do read their works but don't see the point? How many people have to see the point of their works to make their life having been worth being lived?

How many lives are the equivalent of the circumscribed lives of the wives of the Sultan, lived within four modest rooms with high ceilings and a never-changing view of the water? Is this view more interesting than a view of other water for knowing it's the Bosporus? Or the other rather unprepossessing shore interesting for knowing it's Asia? Or the fact that they were, after all, wives of the Ottoman Sultan? Or is it as meaningless as all of the Emma Bovaries who, lacking Emma's fanatical devotion to attaining unattainable goals, simply accepted their drab husbands, drab towns, and drab lives until they died?

Perhaps our horror at seeing these too-high, too-plain rooms in the midst of opulence, the never-varying multi-million-dollar view, is realizing that these people had it all, and yet had nothing. If they had nothing, we may reflect, then what do we have? Perhaps the horror we sense on looking at their heart-breakingly high-ceilinged rooms with their unvarying view of water and the houses on the other shore is looking around us and seeing our own worlds, perhaps on the surface of it more various and interesting, and seeing them as identical to these rooms: this, in thirty, or forty, or fifty years, is where I will die, after having eaten X number of times, gone to the bathroom Y number of times, having begotten (if lucky) Z number of children. Perhaps the horrible aspect of prison is simply the predictability, knowing that every day will be the same, and the day after that, and the year after that, and the decade, and the next. But isn't this our life?

Background and Foreground

The aesthetic sense allows us to consider the philosophical givens of the world we live in collectively, what we call modernity. It also allows us to consider the practical givens of our contemporary lives. Patterns to our lifestyle become clear, typically, when we have something to compare them with—which usually means, when something goes wrong. In the same way that "people don't appreciate good health until they lose it," we rarely see the givens of our lives until these are disrupted. Being aware of these patterns as they emerge, teasing them out, is the aesthetic sense of life.

As, for instance, when the electricity went out. I can put it this way because I know that electricity comes to the house through wires I see strung by the sides of the roads. Most adults are aware of this, but children aren't. If I were a child I would no sooner be able to give this short version from the outside than I would be able to diagnose as illness X or Y an unexplained feeling of tiredness, or internal bleeding. Alternately, I might live in a place that's so frequently subject to power outages that this is something I take for granted as part of the fabric of life, as I take for granted the fact that periodically the car has to be filled up with gas to make it run, or have its oil changed. In retrospect, in fact, it seemed not so much surprise that the electricity had gone out that was the appropriate response, but a weary feeling of "of course": we should almost have expected it. After the fact, it seemed logical that this snow would have caused the problems. We live in a wooded area that hadn't had a big snowstorm in a while; it stood to reason the branches had grown back up since the last time anyone had had to be aware of them. It was wet snow that began as rain; perhaps this froze on branches and the weight of the snow took them down.

But all this was after the fact, as after an accident that happens so fast you have no idea what hit you, or what you hit: only in the aftermath of things can you untangle the skein that didn't seem tangled, and figure out what happened. Indeed, had the neighbor with the four-wheel drive not been obliged to go out and had he not phoned back the report of branches down, I might not have known exactly what had caused the problem for days. As it was, general knowledge enabled me to say "the electricity is out," and blame the snow.

Articulating disruption

Like all changes that affect routine, the electricity being out was something I only articulated slowly. I awoke that morning to a sense that I was colder than usual; I pulled the blankets up and went back to sleep. Later, when the sun had come up I got out of bed and tried to turn on a light in the bathroom: nothing. Then I understood. Still, it didn't seem to me like a major disruption in routine. The few times when we'd had power outages they had been quite temporary. I figured that by the time the rest of the family was up we'd be back in business. In the meantime making do was more a game than anything else.

We have no backups for power outages in the form of propane stove or non-electric heater; our house is on a well with a pump, so that no water came from the faucets and, past the first flush, none went down the toilets. I began to think in order: what would I normally be doing at this point? The answer was, drinking my morning coffee. That wouldn't work either, given that the coffee pot was plugged into a dead socket.

And then, I had an inspiration: my coffee maker was one my wife had bought me that kept its hot water hot all the time. Coffee was instantaneous—I added cold water to replace the hot that flowed out and there it was. If the electricity hadn't gone off too long before, the water should still be, if not hot, at least warm. And it seemed like a victory when the coffee that came out was at least several shades warmer than tepid and I had coffee to drink, albeit far from ideal. The temperature of the water suggested that the electricity had been out for some hours—as was corroborated by the coolness of the house.

I knew enough not to open the freezer, but as it was cold outside I figured that things in the refrigerator could be put out on the porch, if need were. So I got milk and a bowl of cereal. At least the fireplace burned wood, I reflected. I made and lit a fire, though as I consumed the cereal, I decided not very much heat was reaching the other side of the room. As for the tropical fish, their life or death would be determined by how long the electricity stayed off, something I couldn't control. At that point, however, I was still being optimistic: surely this wouldn't last for long.

I tried to go through the things we normally did, categorizing them into "can do" and "can't do." We could breathe, dress, eat, and use the toilets. We couldn't get water, flush the toilets, stay warm without getting dressed in multiple layers or cook complicated food past left-overs. It was like looking at things from the outside, as if a Martian, all actions spread on the table and re-classified rather than merely being things in one path or another we didn't think about—or like packing for a trip, where it's necessary to visualize all the things one will do and get the pajamas, bathrobe, swim suit, and multiple socks that ordinarily we wouldn't have to think about as either we don't use them in our normal lives or they're ready to hand and don't have to be thought about.

The family awoke. We discussed the situation, dressed the children warmly, determined that we weren't getting out of our driveway that sloped up to the road, told the children not to flush the toilet—which they apparently understood as saying *to* flush the toilet. The contributions were going to pile up no matter what: we hadn't stored water to flush the toilets, and it was only later that someone told us we could drain the hot water heater to get water for such things. And then we got on with our lives, knowing that we could at least dress them in their multi-layered snow clothes and go out to play: this was a first large snowfall that Owen, 3, remembered, and a real first for his younger brother.

At this point we still didn't know why the electricity was off, though we remembered seeing what had looked like lightning in the middle of the night, when we had both been awakened by strange noises outside:

later we heard that a "transformer had blown up," though we did not know what this meant. To say that it was "the snow" was the closest we could come, the way you decide that that tired feeling is "something going around,"

I realized I could heat leftovers for lunch in the fireplace: we had a pot that could be put directly in the fire, and I found a way to remove its rubber handle-guard, which otherwise would have melted and gone up in stinking smoke. We finally got the telephone to act normally. The alarm system had begun to hemorrhage in some odd way; there was a high-pitched ringing we almost thought was imaginary until we left the room it was strongest in and suddenly the world was mercifully silent. We managed to get through to the alarm people, who informed us it was the backup battery, and told us how to disconnect it.

We did go out to play in the snow; this was only a moderate success, as our snowman was at best rudimentary and the children's hands got cold despite their gloves, little blocks of red ice protruding from multiple layers of puffed clothing.

And the day wore on. We had several gallons of water in the basement, which tasted funny. Bathing was out of the question; this early in the day in any case it wasn't an issue. We established contact with the neighbors, heard about the tree branches, discussed the extent of the outage—extensive, so we concluded that the electric company had to know about things. But what if everyone thinks that way? we asked. I called the number in the telephone book (it was Sunday) and got a recorded message saying to call back during business hours. Clearly nothing was going to happen today.

At 5 we ate, more leftovers warmed in the fireplace; they were almost depleted. We had candles lined up, but had resolved to put both ourselves and the children to bed early. There were extensive discussions with Owen about why the video machine didn't work: he accepted "it takes electricity" the way a religious believer would have accepted "God doesn't want it to be so" as an explanation. There was enough stored juice in the electric toothbrush to make tooth brushing normal, and with the aid of candles we were in bed early. We had gotten through the day.

The next day was colder: the house had continued to cool in the night. I didn't even look to see how the tropical fish were doing. I moved the remaining contents of the refrigerator to the porch, lit a fire again, brought in more wood to keep it going during the day, and checked the status of the driveway. It didn't seem possible we would still be here later that day.

And yet we were, using up the available food, the excrement thickening the little bit of water in the toilets, the chill growing more intense. By now the driveway was passable, and the ploughs had passed in the road. We went to work, both of us feeling sticky because of not bathing—late the day before I had heated enough of our precious water in a pot in the fireplace to take a sort of sponge bath—I slathered my hair with gel and hoped I was presentable in a suit; I'd shaved that night before; perhaps the students would think it was a "look," this half-stubble.

But our available resources were used up: no more food, the chill in the house to the point where I wasn't sure we could dress the boys warmly enough, or for that matter ourselves, the toilets beginning to stink, the water running out. At work my wife made a reservation for that night at a local motel: it was the last room available, and quite expensive for a chain motel. Everyone else, it seemed, had the same idea, and many people had moved to hotels the day before. I had persisted in my belief that the electricity, the basis of our lives, was going to come on the next minute, and kicked myself mentally when, the next day, I saw that the wires were indeed, as we had heard, dragged down by branches, untouched now for almost two days with no relief in sight. Perhaps I should have been thinking in terms of weeks rather than hours, or even (at my most optimistic) minutes.

Still, we could go to the motel, after going out to eat. We were simply abandoning ship, walking away from a hideously expensive shell, no longer a machine for making living possible but merely four walls and a roof—some protection against the wind, but with time, none against the cold, as if the house were an expensive machine that a single missing screw had caused to shudder, be silent, and become completely useless, waiting now for Nature simply to take over, as it would in due time.

That night, the hotel: the next day, my mother's house. And when we got home the heat had been on since noon, as we knew it had by talking with the neighbors. Most of the fish were dead, but some were still swimming. I removed the bodies with my fingers, flushed the toilets, and turned off the lights whose switches we had toggled without effect two days before and left, without knowing we were doing so, in the "on" position. We ran the dishwasher, full of dirty dishes, and continued with our lives.

Lives out of joint

During this period, automatic actions had become problematic, things we had taken for granted had come to the foreground and become challenges by themselves, many of which we simply lost. Getting clean was no longer the automatic background action that served as a means to other things; it had become the main thing. How to get hot water? I figured out I could remove the rubber cover from the pan's handle and put it in the corner of the fireplace next to the burning wood. In a few minutes the water was boiling; I diluted it with some of the stored water we still had—only a few gallons—and took a sponge bath with a cup, squatting in the tub. Were there sources of food beyond the left-overs? Perhaps the boxes of protein bars in the cellar? But we weren't that desperate, yet. Others had food; we could go out to eat once the roads were cleared.

In such situations, background becomes foreground. This can happen in other ways, when things are suddenly "out of joint" in our lives. Several years before I had stepped off a curb and, within 24 hours, developed a leg cramp so severe it took me literally five minutes to ease myself out of bed. I could barely drive. I dragged myself to the doctor and was misdiagnosed as having a pulled something. But as an added insurance, the doctor gave me a prescription for some physical therapy. Within hours I had dragged myself to the therapist, who told me I had pulled nothing. He worked on me and after a single session I was considerably better. After three sessions it seemed like a bad dream, evaporating into the morning. That, I thought, must be what it feels like to be old, where even normal motion becomes problematic. Or infirm, or ill—all words we use to describe this strange inversion of background and foreground.

Yet inversion isn't the right word either. The strangest thing was to realize that until it comes to the fore, background does not in a sense even exist: that's the taken-for-granted part. The ability to brush teeth, flush the toilet, get food out of the refrigerator—all these aren't the main show, only things that allow the main show.

What such inversions suggest is that we need the aesthetic sense of life to broker the alternation between foreground and background. The aesthetic sense of life involves the realization that we're never aware of background until it becomes foreground, which is something we can't predict—that is beyond our ability to line things up and see the whole thing. We don't know what we're not seeing while we're not seeing it. Usually the alterations aren't as temporary, or as abrupt, as those wrought by the snowstorm. The alterations of time, that change us from blooming twenty-year-old into creaky eighty-year-olds counting every step—as I counted every step with the muscle spasm that only lasted a week—usually come so gradually we simply take them for granted. Or we complain about them, but what is anyone to do? They're part of life.

No certainty is possible, it seems, not even the certainty of uncertainty—the lesson, if there is one, of the line-up of subjective points of view so dear to the early twentieth century, Modernism, Joyce and Faulkner—for we can't label what we don't label. We only label it when we label it. So how to know that there is a vast manifold of things we take for granted that can in their turn become the main show? Only in moments of abrupt reversal like the snow storm, which leaves us feeling that at any moment the world we know can simply be wiped away.

The aesthetic sense acknowledges that certainty is something that contrasts to uncertainty, but that having certainty itself can never be certain—we can't be certain about certainty. It acknowledges that the things we focus on are the things we are focusing on now, with no opinion about whether or not we will always be focusing on them. It acknowledges that the world can be turned upside-down, and says that we will find a way of coming to terms with it. Not necessarily immediately, but ultimately—and many years may pass between these two stages. We fight for everything we have, and can lose it. But then we can get it back again.

Nothing is fixed, except what is: but being fixed means only that we see no reason why it should fail to be fixed. It might nonetheless fail to be fixed. But that too is something we can react to. The aesthetic sense of life, by being reactive rather than active, always has the last word: whatever happens, we can react. It's life-affirming, too: it accepts what happens as part of life.

And what better reason to recommend it?

Chapter Eight
Achieving Goals, Sort Of

THE AESTHETIC SENSE OF LIFE IS an alternative to two extreme views of life with respect to goals, neither of which accurately portrays the reality of things. Both are extremes, and one implies the other. They are the views that a) you can get what you want or b) you can't. The reality is between the two: of course it's possible to get what you want, but only at a certain price, and under certain conditions. It's a deal we have to be willing to make: to get something we have to give something else up. Life is a zero-sum game. Realizing this is the basis of the neither/nor position of the aesthetic sense of life.

We tell children, and ourselves partially believe, that we can reach our goals. This implies having any, but assures us that any amount of striving is the tail of the kite: its meaning, its justification, is at the end. We imagine ourselves running after a moving train: with enough effort we can catch it. Once we've caught it the effort disappears, subsumed into the fact of having caught it: indeed, most of us cease to be aware of it, never asking whether the effort was more than the goal was worth. The effort was then, the goal is now.

The obverse of this is Keats's view, which suggests that though we can catch the object of our exertions, the result is nausea. In the case of the "Ode," the object of exertions is the young woman portrayed on the urn that is the poem's subject, just out of reach of the man. The two are frozen this way for eternity, being after all only carvings on a piece of stone, but the narrator imagines them alive, the boy reaching out to grasp the girl (apparently for obvious reasons), and the girl shrinking away, one of the "maidens loath." The narrator imagines the young man aware of his frozen plight, as if suddenly struck motionless (but not, it seems, thoughtless) on the pot in mid-gesture, like someone abruptly paralyzed by a ray gun or the severing of something vital in the body. We'd assume he'd be upset: he was, after all, about to grab the object of his lust. "Yet, do not grieve," the narrator tells him: he'll always be in love that way, and the girl beautiful ("Forever wilt though love, and she be fair!"). Already it's suggested that getting his object would diminish his feelings. Later in the poem, this is spelled out explicitly.

The love on the urn is what the narrator calls "happy love": it's "forever warm and still to be enjoy'd/ Forever panting, and forever young." It's *to be* enjoyed: it hasn't been enjoyed yet, and for that reason forever panting (with desire, with exertion) and forever young. Contrasted to this is "breathing human passion"—what we see on the urn, frozen eternally and so unable to age, is what I call "urn passion," which apparently is in some Platonic sense "above" human passion—which "leaves the heart high-sorrowful and cloy'd/ A burning forehead and a parching tongue."

The clear suggestion, at least for this part of the poem, is that the frozen unattainable, should we ever be able to get it—though we can't; we can't attain having something be truly unattainable because that's not the kind of creature we are—is preferable to the attainable, because when you get the object of your desire, it turns sour. Your heart is, to be sure, fulfilled: indeed, it's over-fulfilled; it's "cloyed." And then your forehead burns and your mouth is dry.

This suggests that all achieved goals turn bad. A goal is something that, in the language of one of Shakespeare's sonnets, also referring to the object of lust, is "achieved no sooner but despised straight." The aesthetic sense of life rejects this conclusion. At the same time it rejects the motivational insistence we feed the young that goals not only really do satisfy us but somehow justify all the time and effort put into achieving them. Neither this is the basis of the aesthetic sense of life, nor the opposite, the equally strong insistence that achieved goals are like the gold that in the fairy tale turns to ashes in the hands of someone unworthy: they always disappoint us.

The relationship between achieved goal and disappointment is more complex. The strange truth at the center of the aesthetic sense of life is this: sometimes, for a time, we can achieve our goals. But we feel fulfilled only as the result of many things beyond our control. We're like frogs hopping from lily pad to lily pad. If we concentrate on hitting the center of the next lily pad, and in addition are lucky in our aim, we can in fact stay dry. But that's only so if a lot of other things cooperate too: the stem doesn't buckle, no fish bumps us, we don't slip. It can happen. But many other things can happen too. So we can't generalize, all or nothing, about whether we do or do not achieve goals. Sometimes we do, and are fulfilled; sometimes we do, and aren't fulfilled. And sometimes we don't achieve the goal at all—which can lead to us either being sad or philosophical. The only thing that navigates between all these things is the aesthetic sense of life, what unifies them all.

Because the achievement of goals is possibly only under specific circumstances, we have to pay attention to the circumstances. There's no iron-clad rule that works for all. (The demand for a one-size-fits-all rule leads to the disillusionment of the religious point of view.) This is why the aesthetic sense of life is in the middle between an absolute concern with particulars, on one hand, and, on the other, an absolute unconcern with them. You have to pay attention to particulars to see if this is the case where things work out. The aesthetic sense of life means putting on the back burner the very question of whether, in an absolute sense, goals work out or not: what we'll undoubtedly get is a pattern of alternation, not one or the other of the two extremes. The aesthetic sense of life needn't be indifferent as to whether goals are attained or not—clearly attaining is better than not attaining—but it has to understand that fat will probably at some point (only we don't know when) be followed by lean: that's just the way things are. The fundamental currency of life becomes, therefore, not the achievement (or not), but rather the process of moving between the two extremes.

Paris

It isn't true that we can never go—in the Proustian sense—to a place we'd dreamed of going, that where we end up is by definition never the place we'd dreamed of. (For Marcel it was Venice, so enticing as a goal so disappointing in reality.) However actually getting somewhere we'd dreamed of requires fulfilling certain criteria, making careful choices, staying on a certain route, and being lucky. We can do it, but we can't guarantee we'll do it, we can't prolong it past a certain point, and we can't, past a certain point, control it. We go in looking for something; we can in fact achieve it, but we don't know whether or not we will. Realizing this is essential to the aesthetic sense of life: we are conscious of when we succeed and when we fail.

Let's say we'd dreamed of going to Paris. All the things can be exactly the way we'd dreamed of them, or even better: the inside of Notre-Dame is perfumed moving darkness punctuated by candles, lights, the movements of people on the ground, and the droplets of pure color falling from stained glass; Sacré Coeur shimmers in the intermittent sunlight high up on the Buttes-Montmartre; the Bâteau-Mouches glide along the Seine as we stand on the Pont Neuf, looking at the Louvre on one side and the Latin Quarter on the other: of course it can all seem thrilling.

But for how long? We can fill a week with the appointments of the tourist: Today the Louvre, tomorrow the Picasso Museum, lunch at this restaurant, followed by a walk in the Luxembourg Gardens. Being someplace for its own sake, which is the nature of tourism, is an entity with a natural life. It can be longer or shorter, but one thing is certain: it's limited, usually to a few days or at most weeks. Usually we can feel the strangeness seeping out of things, as we look at the silent, plain people in the metro, the cheap clothing in the stores up the Boulevard St-Germain, the piles of trash around the plastic bags that hang like genitals denuded of clothing from the rims of trash-cans removed as an anti-bomb measure: it's all so normal. Our world, the world of the tourist, is only the world of the glittering museum, the shopping on Avenue Montaigne, the major buildings, the quaint side-streets.

And the world of the hotel, whose sole reason for being for the tourist is to make him or her feel catered to: what if instead of "what may I do to serve you?" it's a surly unshaven man at the front desk, finger marks on the wall up the stairs, a tub that doesn't drain properly, and someone else's hair on the badly-cleaned carpet? Our Paris will be a different Paris from that of the person at the Ritz, with its gleaming surfaces, its spotless waiters, and its huge pots of hothouse flowers turning the lobby heavy with perfume. For that matter, an altercation at the airport on arrival can ruin all before we even really start: let's say we are detained and searched, let go only hours later with our pleasant anticipation shattered. If we find a still corner of the so-romantic Seine where the ripples wash against the quai and are trapped and find it full of garbage, Styrofoam cups, plastic bags, and sticks, we can no longer see it the same way as we had while gliding along in our gleaming boat.

We should visit the Place du Tertre in Montmartre in full tourist swing, on a summer night, lights strung from the trees, the sheer number of sidewalk artists making up for the poor quality of their work, every square inch covered with restaurant tables inviting us in. But what if, instead of this, we come too early: the lights do not yet glow against the dark but instead seem to insist forlornly, the shops are empty, full of listless shopkeepers not yet ready for the evening, the restaurant tables not yet set, the afternoon light picking out the trash in the street and the battered store fronts: we have seen too much.

The tourist's Paris presupposes a delicate balancing act of hopping from isolated point to isolated point, like a frog going on lily pads. A local might sniff, saying: "It's not the *real* Paris." But of course it's the *real* Paris: it's real, and it's in Paris. It's an edited version, that's all, edited so as to make the individual feel cosseted as an individual (at a hotel) and pleasantly welcome en masse elsewhere (in museums and sites). These things are strung together to make a day: it can be done, but it's always at the risk of falling apart if we plop in the water rather than on the lily pad. Tourists must stay in their own world if they're to feel welcome in this sense: they do if they remain on the tourist track and if they have money to spend. All arms are open to them. This is an experience that someone who has a great deal of money can sense at home: he or she is welcomed, ushered in, catered to. But at home this person understands that the welcome is for the money, not because of the place. In another place where we're being welcomed because we're not from there, we can have the illusion that the welcome is to us as a stranger.

What differentiates what a local would call the "real" Paris from the tourist's Paris is that typically people who actually live somewhere are not in fact very important: if they are they get no particular thrill from tourism, because they lose their importance, unless it transfers—Princess Diana was no tourist in Paris, for example, or in New York. The famous can't pass unperceived, and so can never have this sense of the solidity of the world outside: this is their curse. To be anonymous elsewhere is the caviar of the middle classes. Pity those who cannot go anywhere on the Earth where they will fail to be recognized, where they cannot merely be a face among other faces passing on the sidewalk. They can never be tourists.

Whooshing about the ears

Yet it's easy to understand why Keats would think we never actually get our goal. While we're involved in working for something, the working for it is actually part of the something in the same way that not-having-it is one of its qualities. When we get it, the aspect of not-having-it is stripped away, and thus the vector arrow of our action. What we achieve is by definition different than what we had before, which was the vector arrow plus a visualization of the goal. While we're exerting ourselves to get the goal, we feel a great whooshing of air about our ears. But like stopping a car we've been riding in, acquiring the thing we wanted causes the whooshing to go away: it wasn't wind, it was merely the air flow produced by the car hurtling forward. There we are in the quiet, all alone. This fact is, it seems, the central one Proust was trying to articulate over many hundreds of pages of *A la recherche du temps perdu*.

But insisting that this means we'll suffer the daily equivalent of post-partum depression when the big event has happened just doesn't jibe with what we experience. Sometimes it does, sometimes it doesn't. In Proust's case, it seems that his expectations were so high they were bound to be disappointed: one of his great deceptions is that the Prin-cesse de Guermantes, whom he had imagined since childhood wreathed in all sorts of historical associations that were part of her family history and colored by his childhood memories, turns out to be an actual person, no more interesting than average, and most horrifying, apparently interested in him. *A la recherche du temps perdu* seems an endless Borscht belt joke, like Woody Allen's self-flagellating quip about "not wanting to be a member of any club that would have him as a member." It's difficult to resist the conclusion that if Marcel had been more adult—not, that is, so loving of his limited childhood perspective that he was able to summon up the memory of his agony over whether mom was going to come kiss him good night—he'd have realized that being an adult means precisely seeing things eye to eye, not looking up to them.

That of course is the point of the book, but a rather dispiriting one— not to mention, I'm suggesting, not true: that the only alternative to the dullness of adult reality is a flight into childhood imagination. But this is circular: the more lurid our childhood dreams and the more we resist allowing them to fade naturally, the greater the deception when we compare them with reality. Most people have allowed them to fade, and this is why most of us avoid the deception of the biologically adult Marcel: the fading isn't sad, it's necessary for survival. Normal people would long before have realized that the Princesse de Guermantes would be a regular person, and if we met her socially, would hope to find her interested in ourselves. We might laugh ruefully at remaining shreds of our fantasy as to what she'd be like, as we might confess to someone we'd dreamed about meeting, after we'd gotten to know him or her well, what we'd thought before meeting him. We're acknowledging that the error was initially ours, in thinking the person would be like that at all. Proust never admits an error: Marcel perceives it like a betrayal—it's the world that's at fault, not he himself.

Trading in the map

If we buy into Marcel's point of view, we conclude that the world is bound to turn sour, let us down. And so we are sent drifting back to childhood, to things that cannot disappoint us, to memories of waiting for mother, of things that to an adult seem so thin as to be nonexistent: a way to come to the house that was called after a person, *du côté de chez Swann*, which was the polar opposite in a child's mind of the *côté des Guermantes*. Most of us give up the maps of our childhood by trading them in periodically. Sometimes indeed a jolt back to the old one will make us rueful: gracious, how small our childhood house now looks! How pokey our old room! Yet there was where lay awake looking at the pattern of the wallpaper, dreaming of whatever we dreamed of, here are the marks from that fight, the pencil marks on the doorjamb where we measured our growth—how we'd forgotten all of that!

Only Marcel hasn't forgotten, and he isn't rueful. He's almost vengeful, Proust's book the working out over thousands of pages of his rage. How dare the world be less interesting than the set of absolutes it appears to be from the perspective of a child! How dare it sort itself out, how dare we grow up to be just those people we once thought so overwhelming, wear our father's suits, and marry a version of our mother in order to have our children (now the story is departing from Marcel's) have their overwhelming vision of the world in their turn that they are required to trade in as they age!—and so on. I have transformed Marcel's fit of pique at the world not being as he'd imagined it into the more usual patterning of the more average person. We all of us go through a trajectory from childhood to adulthood where we come to grips with the fact that now our eyes are not under the sill, looking up and in, but inside, and higher, looking down and out: it belongs to us. The people who once guided us are dead; we're doing the guiding. Typically our third age is that of pleasure at the childhood of our own children, something we can no longer recover for ourselves but can at least enjoy in others.

Perfume

The content of Proust is to say that goals aren't achievable. Proust reacted to this with a sacrifice of which most people are incapable—and which, in any case, is somewhat inhuman. He gave up the future. The result was that he achieved something like the aesthetic sense of life from the direction of the very specific, rather than the more usual direction I'm considering here, ratcheting back from an unsuccessful attempt to achieve the religious. The patterning here, however, is retrospective. Past a certain point no new input is desirable; Proust spends all his time ordering what he has already.

The central scene in Patrick Süsskind's *Das Parfum* (*Perfume*) is an echo of Proust's great renunciation. Süsskind's hero (if that's the right word), Grenouille ("frog") is a runty man with super-human smell capabilities coming to adulthood with the first blush of Romanticism who, true to all Romantic clichés about the artist, himself lacks the qualities of the normal person—he emits no body odor at all, which causes people to shun him without knowing why. Grenouille spends the first part of his life mentally storing up odors and his middle, and central part, all by himself in a cave where, for seven years, he simply "catalogues" and lives off the smells he's gathered in the world. For a time it's enough. What makes Grenouille different from Proust is that he lives too long: he finishes his mental construction and the realizes he must go back into the world for stage three, which involves creating a masterwork perfume from the amalgamated body odor of 24 virgins, whom he must kill in the process. When he douses himself with this essence, the effect is to make the rabble crazed with desire so extreme they tear Grenouille to pieces and eat him. This seems the ultimate act of recapturing not only the past, but the future as well: he has become the future, while at the same time ceasing to exist.

Achieving the aesthetic from the opposite direction

The point of view of the child is largely identical to that of those adults who are on the worldly extreme with respect to the aesthetic sense of life. This book began by describing the aesthetic sense of life as an alternative to the flickering toward transcendence. Proust is the best example of someone who achieved the aesthetic sense by moving from the opposite direction, from the absoluteness of the child's point of view, the focus of someone married completely to the world.

Proust's achievement was to infuse order into the givens of childhood, making more abstract something that had been absolute. His looping back to childhood solved the problem he faced as his absolutes began to seem less absolute: he would redeem their absoluteness by choosing to re-enter his own childhood, this time voluntarily. This re-entering in a voluntary way is what produces the layering of time so central to his "re-finding" time. And this is also what makes him a Modernist: his solution was a solution for himself alone, not for anyone else. The Romantics would have said, they had solved the problem for everyone; the intervening century since the flowering of Romanticism had taught them that this was a vain hope. (See my *Structure and Chaos in Modernist Works* for a more developed form of this argument.)

Proust perceived the world so intensely because he was so marginal to it. We always perceive it so intensely when we're only along for the ride. When we're driving we have to concentrate on the road: there are some things that are intrinsically more important than others, and we can't give equal air time to the also-ran things. We have to prioritize. The intensity of perception of the passenger is that we can simply, idly, notice things. We don't have to rank them.

In the world of the child Marcel, things were merely because they were determined to be that way: he didn't know why. His father had said his mother should not give in to him and kiss him goodnight; he of course couldn't realize that his father was trying to prevent him, Marcel, from becoming precisely the person he was destined to become, someone with no distance from his own wants and desires, no ability to say that in the larger scheme of things, these should be sacrificed to purpose. The *côté de chez Swann* was merely the *côté de chez Swann*: that's what it was, rather than what it was called. Proust's genius as a writer was to make the reader feel the absoluteness of this situation, though the second time through, in a re-created fashion: we are made to sense the absoluteness of childhood, rather than the relativity of things ordered into an adult universe. The writer could only re-evoke this at the second layer, the way the older narrator in Wordsworth's "Tintern Abby" was the only one with the distance on the wild ecstasy of youth necessary to expressing it.

An adult understands why, and so is unable to perceive with the absoluteness of the person who doesn't. This is what Proust rejected: he brought us back to the sense of absolute. This is his aesthetic sense of life, not with respect to the complete blank-out of the religious point of view, but with respect to the absoluteness of the other extreme. The point of view is that of the person who made the funhouse or who slips behind the scene to see the apparatus (the metaphor of John Barth's story of the artist, "Lost in the Funhouse") rather than the person who doesn't know what's coming next. Adults are the scientists in white coats looking down at the rats in the maze. Children are the rats. Proust made peace with being a scientist by becoming a scientist imagining himself a rat.

Jiminy Cricket
The parent who has worked for the money to buy the house, chosen or built this and that, picked wallpaper or counter tops, knows what the world could have been and isn't. What the adult sees is the result of a choice: of course things are this way. I made them so. The child or the outsider accepts these things as being part of the furniture of the world, things they haven't chosen. Typically they remain unquestioned: no one asks, Why have we sat for so long in a chair one of whose legs has a piece missing from the back? Why do we drink from a bowl with a chip? These are the furniture of the world.

Part of the furniture of my world was, for example (each person has his or her own examples), a cup shaped in the head and hat of Jiminy Cricket, the "conscience" from Disney's *Pinocchio.* We got it by collecting cereal box tops and sending away for it. It was in green plastic. The eyes blinked, made of plastic discs with ridges so that from one angle the eye was open, and the other the eye was closed. This cup defined my childhood, even when it became chipped, and when washing caused one of the eyes, which were paper-based, to come off and eventually to be discarded. Mercifully, the world caused this object to disappear, so I have only memories to compare with an adult perspective. If I were to find it now, I would be horrified, I imagine, if tolerant and bemused at the same time: how the cheapest, strangest things, define our lives as children.

And of course the miracle of acquiring it through box tops was not something I could really understand. As an adult, it seems a quaint merchandising trick of the 1950s and 1960s, as odd and now of its time as Green Stamps, which I can see in their books, some pages full of singles, some with the column of tens pasted down the center, never completely within the lines. At the redemption store a clerk wearing a rubber nipple over her (as it invariably was) finger ruffled each page of the book blip blip blip blip to make sure that there were stamps on each page. How we had gone beforehand to check how many books the lamp was, or the toaster, or whatever the object was we were redeeming these for—

The person who invented this system can never see the books with their uneven columns of stamps the way I still can. The factory worker where plastic things like Jiminy Cricket cups were stamped out by hundreds and thousands can never have the relationship to this cup that I still have. Yes, they'd have said if they saw it: we make dozens of those an hour. So what? If you're responsible for it, it can't define your life. Responsibility makes this absoluteness of the world impossible: choosing to have things so rather than another way robs the world of its absoluteness. We have considered other options and rejected them. What we see is an expression of ourselves, not anchored to the world outside.

The price of achieving goals

Proust regained this childhood absoluteness. Most of us find the price for doing this too high: the enclosure in the private world of memory. Still, it was a form of the aesthetic sense of life. So Proust's insistence that it's not possible to achieve goals only "works" if counterbalanced with the determination to order the past, to refuse to bang our nose any more on the world. For those of us who don't turn our backs upon the future, declaring ourselves satisfied with what we have already, such a grand gesture seems simply histrionic, like vowing to hold our breaths until we turn blue. So what if we do? It makes more sense to breathe normally. We come instead to the realization which is necessary to adopting the aesthetic sense of life, that goals are attainable, but at a price.

The first way in which achieving our goals implies a price is this: that in childhood the things we inevitably become seemed far away. Now they're not. We have grown up, and become the people we once looked up to, now finding ourselves looked up to in our turn. Each stage requires a new acceptance. Don't call me Mr. Fleming, a 25-year-old might say to a 15-year-old girl: it makes me feel so old! But he won't say this any more at 50, or perhaps even at 30. And if he is still saying it at 50, we will think him graceless, strange, and out of touch with reality. To whom should a teen-ager say "Mister" if not to a 50-year-old? No one can believe s/he is the one in the mirror with the gray hair and wrinkles. But this was exactly the age at which our parents grew gray and wrinkled; why should we think it was any easier for them than for us? And yet they didn't show it, at least not to us. Nor do we show it to our children, so that when it overtakes them it comes as much of a surprise as it does to us.

The pattern of our life, the fact that we grow into the things that once seemed foreign and fascinating to us, find them banal, and then see them again through the eyes of our children, who find us and our world as foreign and fascinating as we found the world of our parents, may be the best reason for us to cultivate the aesthetic sense of life. One way of looking at it is as a pessimism too deep for tears: adopting it doesn't mean that at any particular point in the developmental process we're sad. It just means that we can't transcend the pattern. Achieving the aesthetic sense of life begins to be possible when we become aware of the normal pattern of our lives without ever being able to live anything but the particular moment we're in.

We come into our own, inheriting the world that before belonged to our parents, exercise that suzerainty over the world we once only dreamed of, and then look around us, wondering why we tried so hard to achieve something that seems so banal. But about that time we are beginning in any case to be supplanted by new people who have yet to realize the fundamentally quotidian nature of the world, something that eluded us in childhood. And as if taking pity on us, nature has it that we begin to lose our strength and begin to drift away, as fundamentally irrelevant to those now in the flush of having taken possession of this world as our forebears were to us as they drifted away. We suddenly understand, but what good does it do us?

Learning more

The premise of George Bernard Shaw's *Back to Methuselah* is that living longer makes us know more. Knowing more will save the human race. But it's not clear that we learn more as we age rather than merely the things appropriate to age rather than youth. In any case it seems doubtful that we can transmit these to the young, or indeed that this would be a good thing if we could. Each person is condemned, or set free, to make the discoveries that he or she must make along the path of life, knowing that they cannot be transmitted and are ours alone: this is the aesthetic sense of life. The point of articulating what happens would therefore be not to save people exertion, or short-circuit things for them, but rather only to articulate for them that others before them have gone through the things that they themselves are going through. It makes them feel less alone, gives them words for things they might otherwise not be able to articulate. But what they get from this is not release from the place where they are, only acknowledgement that traveling this way is the lot of everyone.

In the preface to Wittgenstein's *Tractatus* the philosopher says: Only people who have thought these things themselves will be able to understand this. Only someone who has experienced the thing that's being described can really understand it, and this means: we have to have the thing happen before we can understand. The old are eager to transmit what they call wisdom: this means, the point of view of someone looking back at the pattern of life. But of course this is a point of view the young can't share. What evidence have they that things will be this way for them as well? In any case, knowing that these things are true is as valueless as knowing that they will grow old, and weak, and ugly, and then simply, in the middle of a breath, fade away.

Knowing, and accepting, that at each point in life we are condemned to act out the things that go with that time and place, that position in life, is essential to the aesthetic sense of life.

Believers

The aesthetic sense of life is, to be sure, not achievable for the fiery-eyed "change the world" young, those who really Believe—believe, that is, that things will be better if they do X, Y, or Z. The aesthetic sense of life encourages us to be who we are, do what we do, perhaps rising early to get our day's work done. But it also means that as the afternoon wears on we sit, at least mentally, in a café and watch the world go by, smile tolerantly at the strident or badly dressed people, and look knowingly at the composed, well dressed people. People bound and determined to undertake actions X or Y are certainly going to try them. We too are someone in this world: no position ever removes itself from the world, at least no position short of the position of the saint. We have to know what role we ourselves play, how others see us. So we fulfill our role, and at the same time get pleasure out of watching others fulfill theirs. Our role changes, and we with it: the aesthetic sense of life lets us understand what has happened, the shifting from one pattern to another, even if we have caused the patterns to come to be.

Being committed to a particular role is necessary, but it's not sufficient. Playing a particular role alone keeps our eyes glued to the ground, not at the mid-level implied by the aesthetic sense of life. The world is full of the committed—those who cause most of its problems. These are the people whose reaction to "but what about X?" is to bellow louder, something their adherents mistake for firmness.

This book is not aimed at these people: in fact there is no discussion possible with these people. They know what they know, and it seems absolute to them. Children see the world in this fashion, and we cannot in this sense reason with children. Reasoning means having achieved the possibility of seeing ourselves from the outside, as one of several choices, not as self-evident.

Many people exist who cannot see themselves from the outside; I don't devote much space here to them, if for no other reason that that they don't try to re-conceptualize things by reading books. I note that they exist, are logically as far on the other side of the aesthetic sense of life as those of a religious temperament are on the other, and let it go at that.

The aesthetic sense of life can smile tolerantly at these people: they're part of the world too. Yet they present the more absolute alternative to the aesthetic sense than those on the other side in the scale of abstraction, those with the religious vocation that blanks out all the particulars completely. Those for whom particulars are absolute—which means, their particular particulars—will resist to the death, as insufficiently engaged, those for whom particulars are both real, and generic— the definition of the aesthetic sense. It's unlikely they'll even be able to understand the point of the religious point of view, which is simply too far away from theirs to seem real competition.

Invisible hand

To move to the aesthetic point of view from the flicker of the probably impossible attempt to achieve transcendence in the religious point of view, we need to drop our gaze from the sky to the world beneath our feet, yet not so absolutely that we lose sight of the fact that the world continues on beyond our feet. In the West, where we are taught to be resolute and act, we can achieve this resolution best by distancing ourselves from people who act differently than we do: we have to plow this particular furrow, we come to believe; the world depends on it.

In fact, what the world depends on is many people ploughing many furrows individually. That way the whole field gets ploughed. The intellectual interest of Adam Smith's celebrated notion of the "invisible hand," the market forces that equilibrate all the individual entrepreneurs without their doing anything but following out their personal advantage, is that it offered a justification of this Western "concentrate on your own furrow" view. The more selfish and self-centered you are, the better things are for everyone.

This has turned out not to be true, at least not in narrowly economic terms—and indeed there's no reason to think it would be true, that this is the absolutely best way to create a whole out of individual parts. What it is, is the way least threatening to individuals—which is why it is the theory that those bound to their own furrows are eager to accept, because it solves the problem of "what about others?" without actually making them change at all. The "invisible hand" is the theory of the worldly: do as you do, and things with others will work out. The aesthetic sense of life, by contrast, asks us to glance occasionally sideways at the next furrow, and note that it too is there, as well as to the end of our own lane to remind ourselves that it's there: we know the world is there, and we express the whole by ploughing our own furrow. This knowledge may cause us to change the way we plough the furrow—not sideways, for example, and not so as to make it impossible for others to plough their own furrows. It may make us intolerant too of those who plough furrows that weave in and out, cutting across as they will—much as we may be intolerant of drivers who weave in and out of lanes of traffic. What's the big hurry? we wonder. If everyone did that, we'd have chaos.

The aesthetic sense of life is likely to encourage us to give the collective its due so it leaves us alone—acknowledge the needs of the social, so that, satisfied and appeased, the dog once again lies down and allows us to pass. The aesthetic sense involves a squinting perspective, a focus simultaneously on our own project and the world.

This may be the meaning of Candide's shrug at the end of Voltaire's eponymous novel. There's no way for anyone, including Voltaire himself, to contradict the novel's hapless fall-guy Dr. Pangloss, who insists in the midst of wars, earthquakes, pestulence, and rape, that "this is the best of all possible worlds." By definition it is. Even after Candide has gone through all these misfortunes, as well as seeing his love interest Cunegonde turn from a plump young girl into a shrill and ugly old woman, all he can say to Pangloss's insistence that all these things had to be (because they actually happened) is this: "That may be. But we must cultivate our garden." The cultivation of gardens here echoes my metaphor of the furrow: whatever we decide about the universe as a whole, we fit into it by being who we are. We cultivate our own garden as a way of fitting into the world, as well as a way of answering its call: that's how we fit into it, by being who we are.

Changing the course

The most laudatory thing some of us can say of someone is that he or she has "changed the course of human history." But what does it matter if the course of human history gets changed or not? For every moment of change there are an infinity of others where they're not changing, and we see nothing wrong with these either. Anyway change isn't necessarily for the better. We think the twentieth century is the beginning of progress, say, and then it delivers us two world wars and countless smaller ones, not to mention Adolf Hitler, Josef Stalin, and Mao Tse-Tung, Pol Pot and countless smaller-fry murderers and torturers.

So it can't just be changing the course of human history that we're aiming at, but changing it for the better. The only problem is, we can't even agree on what "better" is. On some things there's pretty general agreement. We think it's "better" to have anesthetics for operations, to have gone beyond "biting the bullet." Lack of pain is held to be a good thing.

But is less pain actually being inflicted nowadays than before? That's the question that never gets asked, and certainly could never be answered. We can focus on the pain saved in operations, but is there more pain elsewhere? We don't even ask questions like this: our notion of progress isn't with respect to the big picture, but instead with respect to one tiny corner, which we compare to that same corner on another version of the picture. Perhaps mudslides or traffic congestion have added either in great chunks or many tiny increments to the sum of human misery to the point where the little bit we save in operations is insignificant. We have no way of talking about the big picture, answering the question whether people are happier today, less happy, more in pain, less in pain—whatever our point of comparison is. We can say, they live in bigger houses, those that do—and need not even say, what of those who don't live in those houses? We can say, fine, we live in bigger houses. But how does that fit into the bigger picture? We don't know; we can only compare apples with apples, not with oranges, and certainly not with Chihuahua dogs.

Sometimes, we know, solutions carry with them new sets of problems, by definition things we can't have foreseen. Greenhouse gase is the most evident example currently before the public eye, to the extent that it is: many people don't want to consider, much less attempt to address, the problem. It's clear why they don't: we always want to compare X with other X, not with Y. Talking about greenhouse gas makes clear that we only solve specific problems (how can we power industry?), not all problems. We can fail to take account of things that later become clear—and it may be evidence of mental limitation that we don't acknowledge things we'd rather not—but we can't be aware of all the other things in other parts of the carpet, for the simple reason that we can never see the carpet as a whole.

Natural boomerangs like greenhouse gases, things that come back to haunt us, make convenient examples of how solving one set of problems says nothing about other problems, and may even create them: rabbits introduced into Australia to make it "more like England," kudzu introduced into the American South as a groundcover that is now choking everything in sight. We can even put labels on other boomerangs that are a bit harder to process. What of the medical illnesses of civilization? Even if we pass over things like cancer and obesity, perhaps we can consider illnesses of other sorts like boredom: what to do with free time? Or do we even have more free time? Perhaps with rising expectations we simply work twice as hard to get twice as big a house: the house is bad for the environment (cuts down trees, paves over ground, uses electricity) and the stress sends us to the hospital with a heart attack at an early age. How to put all these pieces together into a sense of whether things are, on the whole, better, or, on the whole, worse? We don't even have a scales that would put on one hand huge houses and automobiles for the rich against rising water levels for all (also for the rich, who tend to build their houses on coastlines for the "view")—and these are all physical things. How do we measure (or even establish?) things like boredom and stress?

But these are all physical examples, things people are willing to talk about, and for which there is a forum. For many things in the world, there is no forum of talk at all. For example, where is the forum for those who try to measure the sense of success in our lives against the inevitable failures? What for that matter are we looking for? Parity? Some successes no matter how many failures? More successes than failures? Nobody can tell us; there's no way to know. That itself is the problem: so we continue trying to maximize successes and minimize failures without knowing, even with ourselves alone, whether what we get is good, bad, or indifferent. It is what it is.

Must life always be this flailing about in the dark, with the only alternative being to willingly put on blinders so we never ask the questions that make clear to us we really have no clue about the big picture? Yes. This is why we may be impelled to adopt the aesthetic sense of life. It allows us to talk about these things, cataloguing the shifting of the plates around us without ever denying that we ourselves are condemned to live on the shifting surface.

More unnerving still is the realization that relatively few people can ever get to the point of being unnerved about such abstruse things. The kind of realization I'm trying to articulate here is only for the people who've solved the basic problems of human existence, namely assuring survival, and who have too much time on their hands. It's typically the aristocrats who get bored and decadent, never (so we imagine, anyway: but do we really know?) the peasants, those who work in order to live. Only the people not themselves falling victim to the earthquake can conceptualize and talk about it. The victims don't approach the world with an aesthetic sense: they're too busy dealing with the roof falling in, the house sliding into the gulf that has opened up before them. If the question of what it all means can only be asked by those who, by definition, will be unable to answer it—so that asking it at all is proof it has no answer—what does that say about life? Things like this go into the engaged shrug that is at the heart of the aesthetic sense of life.

Index

About the Author

Bruce Fleming's most recent books in philosophy and current affairs include *Annapolis Autumn: Life, Death, and Literature at the U.S. Naval Academy* (2005), *Why Liberals and Conservatives Clash* (2006), and *The New Tractatus* (2007). *The Aesthetic Sense of Life* is the culmination of a series of titles from UPA that include *Art and Argument* (2003), *Science and the Self* (2004), *Sexual Ethics* (2005), and *Disappointment* (2006). A professor of English at the U.S. Naval Academy, Annapolis, Fleming has received the Antioch Review Award for Distinguished Prose (2005). His first published short story won an O. Henry Award, and his experimental novel *Twilley* was compared to works by Proust, T. S. Eliot, Henry James, Thoreau, and David Lynch. He is a former president of the U.S. Dance Critics Association, and author of a book of dance essays, *Sex, Art and Audience*, as well as numerous books on Modernism and aesthetics. He lives outside Annapolis with his wife and children.